# CONFRONTING UNBELIEF

*Your Soul and the
City of the Great King*

Stephanie Quick

**Confronting Unbelief:** Your Soul and the City of the Great King

Stephanie Quick

© 2018 FAI Publishing

**Cover Design:** Stephanie Quick and Dalton Thomas

**Typesetting:** Devon Phillips and Stephanie Quick

A CIP record for this book is available from the Library of Congress Cataloging-in-Publication Data

**ISBN-13:** 978-1-72382-914-7

"For I will not venture to speak of anything except what Christ has accomplished through me to bring the Gentiles to obedience—by word and deed, by the power of signs and wonders, by the power of the Spirit of God—so that from Jerusalem and all the way around to Illyricum I have fulfilled the ministry of the gospel of Christ; and **thus I make it my ambition to preach the gospel, not where Christ has already been named, lest I build on someone else's foundation**, but as it is written, 'those who have never been told of Him will see, and those who have never heard will understand.'"

Romans 15:18-21

# Contents

# ACKNOWLEDGEMENTS

Julie Clark, Robin Kennedy, and Devon Phillips made vital contributions to this book. I am thankful for their input and grateful for their friendship.

*"Come, I will show you the Bride,*

*the wife of the Lamb."*

REVELATION 21:9b

INTRODUCTION

# TRUTH SURVIVES

# SCRUTINY

"But why?"

Two words that push doctoral candidates, challenge scientists, and torment parents of young children. "But why? Why does _____ work the way that it does? Why doesn't _____ work another way? Why is the sky blue? Why are some dogs not very cute? Why do I have to share my toy?"

Two words that, for many of us, were unfairly discouraged in Bible studies, CCD classes, and other church settings. These questions typically started small when we were young and escalated with our growing cognitive capacities as we matured. "But why did God send a whale to eat Jonah?" "But why was the snake allowed in the garden to begin with—*and it talked?!*" "Why was the cross necessary?" "Why are we put in this position where we can even sin at all?" "Why did God bother with all this to begin with?" "Why do we just 'trust' the inerrancy of Scripture?" "Why not just get rid of the devil?"

When I was nine or ten, I was at a Wednesday night version of Sunday school. My teacher was explaining to us that if we missed one Mass (I grew up Catholic), we'd have to attend one hundred more to compensate for the one we missed. I was bewildered. Math has never been my strong suit, but she had just informed us a week or two prior that humans only use ten percent of our brain capacity, while God uses one hundred percent of His (I'm going to give her the benefit of the doubt that she was speaking figuratively). Still, I had to assume that if I, with all my limited brain function and weak disposition to arithmetic, could clearly see her compensatory math was broken, surely God could see it too, right? Why would He put this kind of bondage upon us?

I asked aloud.

"Don't miss a Mass," she responded.

The class moved on.

Many of us have stories like this. Sadly, many whose questions were discouraged or poorly addressed entered adulthood with very capable brains and severely insufficient answers. In this position, we have three ways to navigate our confusion: abandon the faith (tragically common), settle for accommodations to these questions not found in Scripture (also tragically common), or bring our questions to the Jesus of the Scriptures (I hope this is more common than it seems). I don't believe for a moment that humble and heartfelt questions threaten Him. Truth can withstand scrutiny; falsehood can't. We can find the integrity of a bridge pretty easily—just try to drive a truck across it. It either bears the weight or collapses beneath it. Our worldviews are built by bridges; some are true, and some are not. Often, "Christian consciousness begins in the painful realization that what we had assumed was the truth is in fact a lie." [1]

Jesus is "the Truth." [2] He is like a concrete bridge. He is not wooden; He cannot rot. He is not rickety; He does not sway in the wind. In fact, if "the Lord is the rock," [3] He is necessarily the only thing that can withstand wind from any direction. He does not budge. He is steady, strong, and sure.

We are handcrafted by God in the image of God. Ours is a holy dignity; this makes something like unbelief a terrifying kind of treason. Yet we are not without comfort: He knows our frame, and knows we are made of dust. [4] He is very familiar with our limitations—not only because He made and makes us, but because He entered our human experience from conception to death. [5] In fact, only Jesus has lived the full human experience; the rest of us are still

---

1   Peterson, E. (1980). *A Long Obedience in the Same Direction* [Kindle DX]. Location 340. Downloaded from Amazon.com

2   John 14:6

3   See Psalm 18:2; 31; 46; 19:14; 31:3

4   Psalm 103:13-14

5   John 1:14; Hebrews 4:14-15

waiting for our resurrection. [6] He has limitless compassion for us and responds to our confusion and questions so tenderly. When we need wisdom and revelation to understand something, all we have to do is ask. [7] If it is in our best interest to receive specific information, He will give it. [8] If not, He'll give us something sufficient in the meantime. [9]

What comes into our minds when we think about God is the most important thing about us. [10] If we do not love Him with our minds—our beliefs, our imaginations, and our thoughts—we are not loving Him as we ought. [11] The consequences for this are like any other manifestation of disobedience or disregard for His commands: bondage and death. [12] Our destiny in Jesus is "life and life abundant." [13] We should settle for nothing less, and demand with our days to enjoy the freedom of a liberated mind.

Enjoying this freedom will require the kind of sanctification only available from the hand of the Father through the Holy Spirit by virtue of

---

6    John 1:14; Hebrews 4:14-15

7    James 1:5

8    See James 1:5; Acts 1:7

9    See Acts 1:7-8; Mark 10:38-40

10    Tozer, A.W. (1961). *The Knowledge of the Holy*. New York: HarperCollins, 1.

11    Deuteronomy 6:4-5; Matthew 22:34-40, 46; Mark 12:28-34

12    See Romans 6:23; Galatians 5:1

13    John 10:10

what Jesus achieved on the cross—and it takes time. Good things take time. A liberated mind is worth our pursuit; Jesus deemed it worthy of His blood and will not quietly allow His little lambs to live in bondage. Truly, "it is for freedom Christ set us free."[14]

In His kindness, the LORD has given us a living object lesson to lean on and glean from to give us confidence in who He is and what He is like: the literal and historic city of Jerusalem. Jesus is often referred to as "the suffering Servant," per many of Isaiah's prophecies.[15] Israel, the vessel of the Messiah's introduction to the world, is likewise the suffering nation. Jerusalem is her beating heart. Her controversial election and covenantal peculiarity have long generated the rage and animosity of offended nations, people groups, and Christ-confessing denominations throughout history. They have also led the sons and daughters of Jacob themselves to, like Tevye of *Fiddler on the Roof*, look to heaven and cry aloud: "Could You have chosen anyone else?"[16]

By virtue of divine sovereignty, Jerusalem is "the City of the Great King."[17] She is also the city who "kills the prophets, and stones those who are

---

14  Galatians 5:1

15  Isaiah describes the "Servant of the LORD" in chapters 42:1-4; 49:1-7; 50:4-9, 52:13-53:12

16  Stein, J. (1964). Fiddler on the roof. Retrieved from http://www.script-o-rama.com/movie_scripts/f/fiddler-on-the-roof-script.html.

17  Psalm 48:2; Matthew 5:35

sent to her." [18] The nations have a controversy with Jerusalem. The Church has a controversy with Jerusalem. Satan has a controversy with Jerusalem. God Himself has a controversy with Jerusalem. Yet she is the chosen throne for David's Son, [19] and the last time Jesus saw her, He wept. [20]

She has always been complicated.

Jerusalem serves us with her testimony. We may read her story in the Scriptures and learn about the nature and character of her Great King with confidence in His revealed nature and character—His personality—to understand how He views and deals with us once we are grafted into the Everlasting Covenant forged with Abraham, Isaac, and Jacob. Despite the ongoing "controversy of Zion," [21] she is the testimony and revelation of God to the nations—until the return of the King.

Let us examine seven truths of what God is like by exploring His relationship with this complex and controversial city, destined to be "the wife of the Lamb," [22] "adorned for her Husband." [23]

---

18    Matthew 23:37; Luke 13:34

19    Psalm 2:6

20    Luke 19:41

21    Isaiah 34:8

22    Revelation 21:9; see also Ephesians 1:4; 1 Peter 1:19-20; Revelation 5:6, 12; 13:8

23    Revelation 21:2; see Isaiah 54:5

CHAPTER ONE

# HE DOES NOT LIE TO HER

*"I did not speak in secret, in a land of darkness; I did not say to the offspring of Jacob, 'Seek Me in vain.' I the LORD speak the truth; I declare what is right."* [1]

The record of redemptive history begins with the creation account and God's formation of mankind from dust, bone, and blood. [2] Our Genesis story begins with beautiful and breathtaking scenes of the power of the Word of the LORD. He spoke everything into existence—except us. He verbalized His dream—"Let Us make man in Our Image, male and female" [3]—before taking action requiring humility we cannot imagine. He must condescend just to look at the stars; [4] imagine what it meant for Him to touch dirt and earth with holy hands. "It was good," [5] to be sure, but it was still beneath Him. Yet in making us, He proved He is not afraid of getting into our

---

1   Isaiah 45:19

2   Genesis 1:1-2:25; Ephesians 1:4; 1 Peter 1:19-20; Revelation 13:8

3   Genesis 1:26

4   See Psalm 113:4-6

5   See Genesis 1:10,25,31

mud and mess—we would see that later when an Infant took His first sleep in a manger. [6]

For all the power demonstrated by His Word, it is nothing short of ironic that the integrity of His Word would be the first thing to come under demonically inspired scrutiny. The first question the accuser [7] posed to humanity is the question we ourselves still face day-to-day:

*"Did God really say?"* [8]

"Are you sure you heard Him right? Are you sure that's what He really meant? It doesn't look like it. But can you really trust Him anyway?"

Disbelief is sown by seeds of doubt. I'm not afraid of uncertainty, and I don't think Jesus is worried when we start to ask questions. His concern is consistently the heart asking the questions. "What is man that [He] would be mindful of [us]," [9] yet the One willing to stoop to see the stars shine at night is the One higher and loftier than any other, yet scans the earth for those whose hearts are loyal to Him so He can give them this testimony: His strength is made perfect in our weakness. [10] But before we can hang our hopes on anything, we have to trust that His Word is good for its own weight.

---

6   Luke 2:1-7

7   "Satan" means "the accuser"

8   Genesis 3:1

9   Psalm 8:3-4

10   2 Corinthians 12:9

The psalmist would encourage us thus: "The words of the LORD are pure words, like silver refined in a furnace on the ground, purified seven times"[11]—meaning the Word of the LORD could not possibly bear more weight, integrity, and trustworthiness than it does already.

Scripture gives us examples of people who weighed His Word with humility, and some who weighed it with scorn. He only took issue with the latter, and it wasn't because they wondered. It was because they accused. Let us examine four individuals across two contrasts:

The archangel Gabriel is scripturally recorded to have visited and conversed with three humans: Daniel, Zechariah (father of John the Baptist), and Mary (Jesus' mother). Luke opens his "detailed account"[12] of "the things accomplished among us"[13] with Gabriel's meeting with Zechariah,[14] and immediately follows it with the angel's meeting with Mary.[15]

These two individuals were in two very different positions: Zechariah was in the twilight years of his life, and Mary was barely entering adulthood. Zechariah had spent years serving the LORD as a priest, but Mary was only beginning to bear her assignment and calling before God. Yet

---

11   Psalm 12:6

12   Luke 1:3

13   Luke 1:1

14   Luke 1:5-20

15   Luke 1:26-38

both were receiving the same message: "You're about to have a son." Their reactions sounded similar, but could not have come from farther corners of confidence: Zechariah heard the news not only after years of praying for a son and bearing the shame of childlessness—his community would've seen it as something of a curse or symptom of secret sin—but likely after years of prayerlessness that followed decades of disappointment. In all likelihood, he and his wife Elizabeth were married in mid-late adolescence and prayed perhaps until she hit menopause that they could have children, or even just one child. They never did. Now they were the grey-haired patriarch and matriarch of a community with no one to inherit their home when they passed into glory.

Disappointment breeds disillusionment. Disillusionment paves a smooth road for disbelief. When the word of promise came, Zechariah literally couldn't believe it. He all but ridiculed Gabriel for delivering the message.

> *Gabriel*: [16] "Heaven heard all those prayers, Zechariah. You're not dead yet, and your God is giving you a son. It's going to blow your mind."

> *Zechariah*: "Yeah, well. We've had a few false alarms. How do I know this isn't one of those? Even biology is against us now. Don't taunt me."

---

16    This is my (lighthearted) paraphrase of Luke 1:13-20

*Gabriel*: "I'm not your emotions, Zechariah. I stand in the presence of the One who keeps your internal organs functioning without you even thinking about it, and He sent me here to give you very good news. So we're just going to keep you quiet till the child comes and give you plenty of time to just marvel at His hand in your life. Wait it out."

Conversely, a woman with her whole life ahead of her still held the luxury of naivety. A few months after locking Zechariah's mouth shut (while his wife was already pregnant), Gabriel appears to this young girl not long before she's due to be married:

*Gabriel*: [17] "Mary! Don't let this freak you out, but it's a good thing: you're going to conceive a life in your womb and give birth to a baby Boy. He will be the Son of God and inherit the throne promised to David. [18] The Kingdom coming you've heard about your whole life [19] belongs to Him."

Imagine, now, all the ways Mary could've reacted. How would you have reacted? I probably would've gone through an immediate recall of anything I'd had to drink in the twenty-four hours prior

---

17    This is my (lighthearted) paraphrase of Luke 1:28-38

18    1:32-33; see 2 Samuel 7; Psalm 2; 89; 110

19    The prophets and psalmists all spoke and sang at length about the kingdom appointed to David's Son. It was the expectant hope of Second Temple-era Judaism, and precisely why the apostles thought they were living in the days to see it come in fullness (see Acts 1:6).

or wondered something like *"What was on my pizza last night?"* No doubt she was blinking at him a bit. But she didn't ask for confirmation like Zechariah did. She asked a question that assumed assurance.

> *Mary*: "Well okay. How's He going to pull this off?" She, too, faced her own biological limitations. "I've never slept with anyone."

> *Gabriel*: "Details. That's not a problem, and it's not part of this equation."

> *Mary*: "You tell the One who sent you that I'm His to do as He pleases. So amen, let it be."

Cynicism is a deadly tonic. Zechariah was drunk on it. Mary wasn't. There is something to be said about youth and inexperience—we're not so likely to consider our Father in heaven a liar when we haven't had to navigate the bankruptcies of bitterness and intoxication of disillusionment. We're not so quick to think He tempts us, or sets us up to screw us over. James would later address this accusation head-on: "Blessed is the man who remains steadfast under trial, for when he has stood the test he will receive the crown of life, which God has promised to those who love Him. Let no one say when he is tempted, 'I am being tempted by God,' for God cannot be tempted with evil, and He Himself tempts no one....Do not be deceived, my beloved brothers. Every good and perfect gift is from above, coming down from the Father of lights, in Whom there is no variation or shadow due to change." [20]

Put simply, He does not tease us. He does not taunt us. He does not tempt us. He cannot lie. [21] He can be trusted.

Likely very few people knew Zechariah had such deep roots of disbelief in his heart. They may well have taken him by surprise. He was doing all the stuff. He was literally the priestly representative of the nation when he experienced this exchange. He held an office serving as a type and shadow of how his Nephew would serve him. He was faithful. He kept showing up to work. He sang all the songs, prayed all the prayers. Yet when God made him a promise, he immediately recoiled. He maybe didn't altogether balk, but he stiff-armed the good news.

His resistance to promises betrayed his deep-seated suspicion: God might be a liar.

We see the dark distrust of Zechariah's heart in a woman's as well: a little over three decades later, after Zechariah's son had lost his head to a drunk and spineless king, [22] his Nephew had a thriving ministry throughout the nation. Mary's Son was coming into much of the witness of the coming Kingdom He was born to give. We have no accounts of Him encountering a sick or infirmed person and leaving them in the state

20   James 1:12-13,16-17

21   Numbers 23:19; 1 Samuel 15:29; Proverbs 30:5; Titus 1:2; Hebrews 6:18

22   Matthew 14:1-12

He found them. He literally healed every sick person He met. [23]

So of course, when His friend Lazarus fell ill, his family appealed to their Friend for help. [24]

So of course, Jesus took His sweet time showing up. [25]

Lazarus died. [26]

And Jesus wept. [27]

Then He pulled the dead man out of the grave. [28]

But some things occurred between Lazarus' last breath and Jesus' suffocating tears: when He arrived a few days after the man's body had been locked in a cave behind a heavy stone door, grief had cloaked Martha's eyes. The Gospel authors give us a bit of background before we meet her here, [29] but it is enough to say we know she lived with a burden that had already blinded her to the beauty of Jesus. [30] Her sister didn't. So when He showed up after they'd buried their brother, they each said the same thing:

---

23   Matthew 4:24; 8:14-16; 9:2-6; 18-35; 10:8; 14:14,35; Mark 1:32-34; 5:41; 6:5, 13,55-56; Luke 4:39-40; 7:2-10

24   John 11:3

25   John 11:6

26   John 11:11-14,17

27   John 11:35

28   John 11:43

29   Luke 10:38-42

30   Luke 10:41

"Lord, if You'd been here, my brother wouldn't have died." [31] Martha leveled her accusatory bitterness at Him. Mary simply grieved. Both knew the resurrection was coming, but Mary's ability to keep an open heart to the Word of the LORD [32] let the penny drop for her that day. She knew almost immediately Jesus would have to come out of His own grave to bear Lordship over everyone else's. [33]

Lazarus' resuscitation secured Jesus' crucifixion. [34] Our LORD does not make a claim upon something He has not ordained. "The Son of Man is the LORD of the Resurrection." [35] He could comfort Mary and Martha both with this doctrine because He knew He'd made a decree: the Son of Man would die and be resurrected as a first fruit of many more to come. [36]

Here we find the foundation of the faith we confess: the coming resurrection of the dead. [37]

Hope for life after—moreover, out of—the grave was the anchor of Abraham's confidence in the God who beckoned him into offensive

---

31    John 11:21,32

32    See John 1:1-5,14

33    Matthew 12:8; 26:12; Mark 14:8; John 11:25; 12:7

34    Bloom, J. (2018). Why Jesus wept. Retrieved from https://www.desiringgod.org/articles/why-jesus-wept

35    Matthew 12:8

36    Romans 8:29; Colossians 1:18; 1 Corinthians 15:20-23; Revelation 1:5

37    See Daniel 12:2,13; Luke 24:1-51; John 11:23-25; 1 Corinthians 15:3-8; Hebrews 11:17-19

obedience. [38] It was the only reason he was willing to bring his promised son up Jerusalem's ominous hill; it was the reason why this boy born by covenant carried his own wood to die on up the incline. Heaven's commitment to this promised end is why an angel intervened and stopped the hand of the covenantal father from wielding its blade; the LORD would indeed provide Himself a lamb. [39] Moriah, that fateful day, saw only a ram. [40] Good things take time, and this was but the beginning of the revelation of God in this age of Gethsemanes and Golgothas. Indeed, the resurrection of the saints is altogether bound up to the arrival of the Great King to His Eternal City, when He breaks every bow and melts every sword, ends every war and fully restores the created earth. [41]

Jerusalem's future grace was alluded to on Moriah, spoken of in Gethsemane, and secured on Golgotha. The "Place of the Skull" [42] would see the Son destined to rule the children of Jacob who'd crafted a golden calf in Sinai. [43] Gabriel did not visit Zechariah or Mary simply to dole out birth announcements; life did not lay hold of barren or virgin wombs simply to

38   See Genesis 22:1-18

39   See Genesis 22:8

40   See Genesis 22:13

41   Psalm 46:8-10; 110:5-7; Isaiah 2:1-4; 9:7; 11:1-10; 42:1-4; Micah 4:1-5; Revelation 21:3-4

42   Matthew 27:33; Luke 23:33

43   Exodus 32:1-8

display the might of Heaven's hand—though display it they did. The archangel visited men and women to speak of the "Messenger of the covenant,"[44] and the man who would prepare the people of the covenant for what He would say.[45] While pregnant with David's promised Son, Mary visited Elizabeth—then pregnant with Zechariah's promised son—and declared this: "God has helped His servant Israel, in remembrance of His mercy, as He spoke to our fathers, to Abraham and his offspring forever."[46] Her confidence in the faithfulness of her Maker was traced back before David, back through the wilderness, beyond the stone tablets bearing His commandments, before the Red Sea, all the way to the hills of Hebron.[47] He made promises to Abraham, Isaac, and Jacob; a Son of Judah would emerge from Bethlehem to rule and reign.[48] The Seed promised in the shame of Eden's aftermath was about to take His first breath in the Promised Land[49] "to show the mercy promised to our fathers and to remember His holy covenant."[50]

---

44    Malachi 3:1

45    Isaiah 40:3-8; Luke 1:16-17

46    Luke 1:54-55

47    Genesis 13:13; 15:1-21

48    Genesis 49:8; Psalm 60:7; 108:8; Micah 5:2; John 7:42

49    Genesis 3:15

50    Luke 1:72

Our ability to believe for our own future grace five millennia or five minutes from now hinges on the depth and degree of integrity we believe the Word of the LORD to hold. Jerusalem confronts us with Satan's four slanderous words like little else can, and illustrates to us the living veracity of her King's commitment to her good;[51] truly, if He can keep His Word to her—to make her clean and be her King[52]—He can achieve the smaller tasks of keeping His Word to the likes of you and me. He must: our hopes are bound and yoked to the people, nation, and land of Israel, represented by the holy and defiled city of Jerusalem. If He *doesn't* keep His Word to her, He cannot and will not keep His Word to us.

But He has kept His Word to her, and He will continue still. As we read the promises in the pages ahead, let us lean with gratitude on this ancient tree we are humbly "grafted into"[53] and glean the confidence due His inerrant and infallible Word.

He does not lie.

He does not lead astray.

He seeks, pursues, invites, and saves.[54]

---

51    Jeremiah 32:40-42

52    Psalm 48:1-2; 99:1-2; Isaiah 1:18; 24:23; 27:9; 40:2; 53:6; Jeremiah 23:6; 33:16; Micah 4:7; Zechariah 3:1-5

53    Romans 11:16-25

54    Psalm 7:10; 23:6; John 3:14-16

We can sleep at night knowing we will not run this race in vain. [55]

---

55    2 Timothy 4:7; Hebrews 12:1

CHAPTER TWO

# HE FIGHTS FOR HER

*"The LORD of hosts will come down to fight on Mount Zion and its hill. Like birds hovering, so the LORD of hosts will protect Jerusalem; He will protect and deliver; He will spare and rescue [her]."* [1]

If "greater love knows none than" giving your life for your friends, what do you call spending your life on your enemies? [2] This is a love foreign to hearts governed by iniquity and beholden to darkness—and such were we. [3] This love is foreign to us, but it is the love we're meant to learn. Amy Carmichael called it "Calvary love," with so many examples of why she knew nothing of it. [4] Yet Jesus intervenes in our lives with His, loving us such that we are able to love Him back. [5] His is a costly affection wrought with unflinching covenantal allegiance soaked with the kind of blood, sweat, and tears that saturated Golgotha and Gethsemane. Not content to leave us to the fatal consequences

1   Isaiah 31:4-5

2   John 15:13; Romans 5:8

3   Romans 1:21; 1 Corinthians 6:11; Ephesians 4:18

4   Carmichael, A. (n.d.). *If.* Fort Washington: Christian Literature Crusade.

5   1 John 4:19-21

of our own selfish decisions, [6] nor to leave us victims to the crimes committed against us, [7] His goodness and mercy hound us down and find us out [8] with such fervency and devotion that His love for us can be so well described as "reckless." [9]

Yet we are not objects of His affection because we were particularly dazzling enough to catch His eye, and Israel certainly wasn't either. [10] As He set the stage to reveal Himself to the nations, He began with one requiring His architecture from the ground up, having appointed a childless man and barren woman to give birth to a family of tribes who would, in time, be known by a name of their father: "He who fights with God." [11]

Israel.

She has been struggling to survive since she began. "On the day you were born your navel cord was not cut, nor were you washed in water to cleanse…no eye pitied you, to do any of these things for you, to have compassion on you; but you were thrown out into the open field, when you yourself were loathed on the day you were

---

6    Romans 6:23

7    Deuteronomy 32:35; Romans 12:19; 1 Thessalonians 4:6; 2 Thessalonians 1:8; Hebrews 10:30

8    Psalm 23:6

9    Asbury, C. (2017). "Reckless Love." On *Reckless Love*, audio. Redding: Bethel Music.

10   Deuteronomy 7:6-8; 1 Peter 2:9

11   Genesis 32:27-28

born." [12] Every odd was stacked against her survival. She was ill-equipped to save herself. Yet "when I passed by you and saw you struggling in your own blood, I said to you in your blood, 'Live!' Yes, I said to you in your blood, 'Live!'" [13]

Jesus' intercession both conceived and kept this fledgling nation; Abram would've stayed in northern countries had he not received the call to wander, [14] and he would've died without a biological heir if not for Heaven's miraculous hand verifying the covenant cut on the hills of Hebron. [15] Even then, the children destined to "outnumber the stars" were also determined to spend four centuries under the oppressive hand of slavery. [16] Their time in Egypt would come and end just as it had been ordained, and He would lead them through the Red Sea and Sinai to make it to the land promised to their father Abraham. [17]

They would resist.

Wrestle.

Rebel.

Accuse.

---

12   Ezekiel 16:4a-5, NKJV

13   Ezekiel 16:6, NKJV

14   Genesis 11:31-12:5

15   See Genesis 13:18; 15:1-20

16   Genesis 15:13

17   Genesis 15:15; Exodus 13:17-15:21; Joshua 1:1-9

"The LORD hates us! He has brought us out of Egypt to destroy us in the desert."[18]

*How quickly we can lose perspective.* How quickly do we descend into delusional accusations against His goodness?

It's important to read their story—Israel and the LORD's—knowing two things: One, it was initiated and is kept by the latter, and was impossible and often ignored and blundered by the former. Meaning Israel is only still an entity today because she still matters to Jesus. He yoked Himself to her. Second, He's after her heart. That's why love is the greatest command and loving Him with everything she has are the only terms allowed.[19] He never wanted a ritualistic relationship for the sake of checked boxes and good grades[20]—though the rules and rituals were given as tutors and governors before Immanuel's flood washed us up well enough for Him to dwell in and guide those who call upon His name.[21]

Often times, He will offend the mind to reveal the heart. He'll press His little flock and small sheep into uncomfortable territories with challenging circumstances or the fire of trial or the stress of persecution. Even when we proverbially take the dry path through the Red Sea and turn around

---

18    Deuteronomy 1:27

19    Deuteronomy 6:4-5; Matthew 22:34-40, 46; Mark 12:28-34

20    See Psalm 51:16-17; Isaiah 58:5-9; 66:1-2

21    See Galatians 4:1-7; Colossians 2:17; Hebrews 8:5

to watch it swallow our enemies—a pretty clear illustration of deliverance and favor—we can ourselves be caught off-guard that such latent unbelief was buried so deeply in our hearts. But Jesus is never caught off-guard. We are our own blind Bartimaeuses, [22] and He will "help our unbelief."[23] When He does, He will chase every "little fox" out of the gardens of our hearts and rip out every devouring weed. [24] It will often sting, but there is a sweeter comfort in the fires of His jealousy[25] than the fleeting counterfeits and gnashing consequences of unbelief. [26]

His jealousy is not narcissism or abusive insecurity. It is His covenantal fidelity and unwavering commitment to do His wife *good*. [27] He is a good Husband, and this is the testimony of Scripture. What we could call the "bridal paradigm" of Scripture is apparent from beginning to end; even as Paul wrote of Adam's death-inducing disobedience, he referred to the first man as "a type of Him who was to come."[28] How could Adam's destructive disobedience by which we

---

22   Matthew 20:29-34; Mark 9:46-52; Luke 18:35-43

23   Mark 9:24

24   Song 2:15

25   Exodus 34:14; Deuteronomy 4:24; Proverbs 6:34; 8:6-7

26   Matthew 8:12; 13:42,50; 22:13; 24:51; 25:30,41; Luke 13:28; Revelation 21:8

27   Jeremiah 32:40-42

28   Romans 5:14

all now die serve as a "type," or a "shadow" of Jesus' obedience that brought us life? [29]

Let us return to our Genesis and revisit the familiar story of the earliest Garden. A man awakes from a covenant with a scar in his side, only to find his rib was used to form his long-awaited companion. [30] "Bone of my bone; flesh of my flesh." [31] *We are one, and we belong together.* When his bride crossed the threshold from allegiance to treason, light to dark, life to death, Adam would have felt it. (Can't you? You know when something has shifted in your friend or lover's heart, do you not?) In a sin of self-reliance and heeding a voice besides his Maker, [32] he went in after her. Our human disposition to stray from our Maker and betray our own origin was exposed in a moment over a hollow taunt to take what we already had— likeness to God. [33]

How could this be like Jesus? When the LORD found them hiding under leaves known for causing rashes, everyone answered His questions honestly. Maybe they were trying to point fingers and shift blame, but the woman and the man both came clean. "I was deceived," confessed she. (Yes, girlfriend, you were.) And him? *"The*

---

29   Romans 5:12-17

30   Genesis 2:7-9; 15-25

31   Genesis 2:23

32   Genesis 3:17

33   See Genesis 3:5 (temptation) in light of Genesis 1:26-27 (truth).

*woman You gave me did the thing I knew would kill her, and I followed her."* [34] Why? *Because she was his.* Could Adam save her? *No.* That's not the point of the story.

The point is that Jesus could.

"The Lamb slain before the foundations of the earth" [35] entered time and space at just the right moment [36] to dive six feet deep into the grave of our own making and infidelity to rescue the bride formed from the blood and water pouring from His rib. [37] She is Jerusalem, [38] and by the finished work of Jesus at the Place of the Skull, she is us [39]—and we are her, but all our hopes and ransom hinge upon His fidelity and faithfulness to Jerusalem. We can *only*— tactfully—read ourselves into the story in light of being grafted in so that His name would be famous among the nations. Jeusalem is the pedestal, the true "city set on a hill" [40] to beam the life of His light into the rest of this dark and disbelieving world. [41]

---

34  See Genesis 2:16-3:6

35  Revelation 13:8

36  Ephesians 1:10

37  See Genesis 2:21-22; Matthew 27:24

38  Isaiah 54:5; Ezekiel 16:1-8; Hosea 1:1-3:5

39  Galatians 4:21-31

40  See Isaiah 60:1-3; Matthew 5:14-16

41  See Romans 1:18-2:16; Ephesians 2:1-3

So great is His commitment to the life and freedom of His wife, it is beyond what we can imagine or inherently believe. [42] So He came to a man with a name not unlike that of the Son of Man, [43] and told him to marry a woman who loved promiscuity over covenantal fidelity so that this man (and his nation through him) could understand a measure of what Israel puts the LORD through. What Jerusalem puts Jesus through. What we put Him through.

And so we can see a measure of what He sees *us* through.

We can only forfeit delusion for truth when the truth is revealed to us, and the LORD goes to war for our hearts and minds by targeting and combating the lies we believe—about the world, about ourselves, and about Him. If He can keep covenant with Jerusalem, He can keep covenant with anybody. She is the Gomer after whom He must "go again," and "go again," and "go again," and "go again." [44] She is the one He must surround with thorns to provoke and fire to protect. [45] Our only tangible confidence that He will doggedly pursue us till Kingdom Come is that He has not yet given up on Jerusalem. This is our holy reassurance that even when we

---

42  See Ephesians 3:20-21

43  See Numbers 13:16; Hosea 1:1-2; Hosea was also the original name of Moses' successor Joshua ("Yeshua," or what many of us call "Jesus"). "Hosea" means "salvation;" "Joshua" means "YHWH is salvation."

44  Hosea 1:2; 3:1

45  Hosea 2:6; Zechariah 2:5

squander our lives, [46] make our bed in hell, [47] or bear a man's children while we bear the name of Another [48] that *He will track us down*. He is the "hound of Heaven." [49] She is the Peter denying Him over and over and over until the day breaks and shadows flee, for whom He'll go to war to vindicate, [50] and we are just like Peter, just like Jerusalem. And happily, we are not big or strong enough to sway Him from who He is—and He is the faithful Husband. He keeps His Word. He keeps His covenant. To achieve both, He must also keep Jerusalem, and keep His sheep. [51]

We are His sheep.

---

46   See Luke 15:11-32

47   Psalm 139:8

48   See Hosea 1:6-2:1; of the three children born to Gomer, only one (1:3) is specifically identified as Hosea's child. The command to not "take" or "bear" the name of the LORD (see Exodus 20:7; Deuteronomy 5:11) has less to do with what erupts from your mouth when you stub your toe and more to do with the fidelity of your affections and allegiances to the One who ransomed you from death with His own blood.

49   Thompson, F. (1893). *The Hound of Heaven*.

50   See Isaiah 31:4-5; Zechariah 14:3-9

51   Psalm 78:52; 79:13; 100:3; 119:176; Jeremiah 50:6,17; Ezekiel 34:11-22; Matthew 9:36; 10:6,16; 15:24; 18:12-15; Luke 15:3-5; John 6:39; 10:1-18,26-27; 18:9; 21:17; 1 Peter 2:25

CHAPTER THREE

# HE FORGIVES HER

*"I, even I, am He who blots out your transgressions for My own sake, and I will not remember your sins."* [1]

To bring a whore back home as His wife, He must forgive her infidelities. To welcome us to the throne of grace when we need help, [2] He must be dripping with such forgiveness that a rain of mercy forms a rainbow around the eternal throne founded in righteousness and justice, [3] or we can't come. The stakes are, for us, as high as the heavens in which He dwells. [4] Even if we *know* in our minds that *technically, yes,* He forgave us at Golgotha and is willing to forgive us still today—or at least when He returns—we don't always feel it in our hearts. John the Beloved encourages us with these old words: "even when our hearts condemn us, God is greater than our hearts and knows all things." [5]

1  Isaiah 43:25, NKJV

2  Hebrews 4:16

3  Psalm 89:14; 97:2; Isaiah 16:5; Revelation 4:3 (the rainbow has been a sign of mercy since Genesis 9:11-17).

4  Psalm 113:5; Isaiah 57:15; 66:1

5  1 John 3:20

How is that enough to let us off the hook? *We* feel the weight of our sin. Doesn't He?

Once again, our confidence in His character is founded and grounded in His mercy and grace for His obstinately wayward wife. The prophet Zechariah received a vision of how the Judge of the earth sees Jerusalem's sinful stains. [6]

It was every sinner's worst scenario.

Jerusalem, here represented by her high priest at the time of the vision (a man named Joshua, but not to be confused with the Joshua who succeeded Moses), stood in a courtroom with God on the bench and Satan in the prosecutor's seat.

Imagine yourself here, because this could be you.

Joshua was, of course, filthy. [7]

But before Satan—literally, "The Accuser," that damned serpent of old—could even begin to launch his case against Jerusalem and against the man responsible for purging her of all her iniquities, before the prophet even noticed in the vision and remarked in his record that the Holy City's high priest was, himself, *filthy*, the Judge intervened:

> "The LORD rebuke you, Satan! The LORD *who has chosen Jerusalem* rebuke you! Is

---

6   Zechariah 3:1-10

7   Zechariah 3:3

this not a brand plucked from the fire?" [8]

*Let Me remind you, devil, this isn't about her.*

Joshua's integrity wasn't at stake in the courtroom. Neither was Jerusalem's. Why? Theirs, in and of themselves, is a closed case. Jerusalem's integrity, in and of herself, is a wanting tale. She is blood-stained and bullet-scarred. So what so aggravated the Judge that He would not even entertain the prosecution's accusations?

It was about *Heaven's* integrity.

He who has promised to make Jerusalem white as snow [9] needs not to be told she is foul and filthy. He who gave her His name in covenant requires no reminders she's going home with other men at night. [10] Satan's case against her is not so flimsy that he needs to point to the obvious. No—he is pointing to the implications. He's dragging Joshua and Jerusalem before the Judge because *the Judge is the One who promised to purify Jerusalem.* Not simply by absolving her sins—but by providing the necessary means to justify her despite them.

C.S. Lewis was not far off the point when he painted Edmund's condemnation for treason. The White Witch approached Aslan to claim her prize—this stupid young boy motivated by

---

8    Zechariah 3:2, NKJV

9    Isaiah 1:18; that this is the heart of God for His people individually is reflected in David's repentance prayer (Psalm 51:7).

10    See Hosea 3:1

his own self-interests—and reminded the ruling Lion of the Ancient Laws. He roared in return:

> "Do not speak to Me of the Ancient Laws. I was there when they were written." [11]

Aslan, of course, would go under the blade of execution in Edmund's stead, destroying the White Witch's claim on his life.

Jesus does the same for Jerusalem.

*"I plucked this brand from fire, devil."*

And Joshua, standing there doing and contributing absolutely nothing to the conversation or exchange, is given white robes in exchange for his filthy garments. He did nothing but stand before his Advocate, and he got cleaned up just perfectly. The case was closed. *The Judge's righteousness was sufficient.* It didn't matter that Joshua's wasn't. It didn't matter that Jerusalem's wasn't. Satan wasn't after the man or the city. *He was after the Judge.* He wants to find a fracture in the throne of heaven to erode it, to usurp it. [12]

This is an important point Jeremiah himself clung to; "the Weeping Prophet" was not unfamiliar with Jerusalem's sins, iniquities, treasons, or infidelities. He saw them. He felt them. They wore on him and wore him down. So why did he weep?

---

11    Lewis, C.S. (1950). *The Chronicles of Narnia: The Lion, the Witch, and the Wardrobe* [Kindle DX version]. Downloaded from Amazon.com

12    See Isaiah 14:12-15; Matthew 4:1-11

Because he knew the promises. He knew what Jerusalem was and is *meant for* in God. He remembered Abraham and Isaac instead of Ishmael and Jacob instead of Esau. [13] He remembered all the nations of the earth are meant to be blessed in her. [14] How could this be possible if she is too foul to come near her Husband?

Jerusalem's confidence, and ours, is this: there is a blood-stained Advocate in the courtroom appealing on our behalf. He took the punishment we deserve so that He could pardon us forever and remain both "just and the justifier" [15] of restored traitors. A restored wife. Our confidence is Gomer's confidence, that we could never be too dirty, or too foul, or too sinful to be redeemed.

Even today, we must live in a world until the rule of David's Son and remember the promises of God, lean on and cling to the integrity of His Word, and trust fully in His righteousness. Jerusalem is still foul and filthy. *She will not always be.* The question isn't whether or not *she* is sufficient; the accusation is whether or not *He* is sufficient. If we dare to call upon her own beloved and broken Son of Promise to deliver us from our own sins, we must stand with and for her in intercession that He will also deliver her from hers. We have no right to spit on or scorn

13    See Genesis 17:1-27; 25:19-34

14    Genesis 12:3; 22:18; 26:4

15    Romans 3:26

her. She is our mother. [16] The apple never falls far from the tree. If Heaven does not wash her white as snow, if she never shines "something like jasper," Heaven will not wash us either and we are of all men and women on the earth the most pathetic wastes of time and breath. [17]

"Who is a God like you, pardoning iniquity and passing over the transgression of the remnant of His heritage?" [18] sang the prophet Micah. Seven chapters of judgment's decree against Israel's covenantal infidelity end with these precious verses:

> "He does not retain His anger forever,
>
> Because He delights in mercy.
>
> He will again have compassion on [Israel],
>
> And will subdue our iniquities.
>
> You will cast all our sins
>
> Into the depths of the sea.
>
> You will give truth to Jacob
>
> And mercy to Abraham,
>
> Which You have sworn to our fathers
>
> From the days of old." [19]

---

16   See Isaiah 54:1-3; Galatians 4:21-31

17   1 Corinthians 15:14-19

18   Micah 7:18a, NKJV

19   Micah 7:18b-20, NKJV

Note the appeal to the patriarchs—You swore truth to the Deceiver (the literal meaning of "Jacob"), and mercy to the father of many nations. This is about Your Word to our fathers, and we are their defiant children. So we trust You to keep Your Word, because we can't.

Micah's hymn is not unfamiliar to many who've spent years in evangelical settings. It is the chorus to popular hymns and worship songs—but it is only true for us who are grafted in if it holds true for the original recipients to begin with. Jacob's priority is not for Jacob's sake, but for the One who claimed and crafted him. [20] Israel's covenantal peculiarity serves our covenantal security. Our righteousness is no longer about us, or Jerusalem, but the Author and Finisher of the faith by which we are cleansed and justified. [21] He is the One who "washes us with the water of His word" [22] to renew and restore us, and His strong and sure integrity laced throughout His holy writ builds our strong and sure confidence in who He is and what He is like.

He is gentle. [23]

He is kind. [24]

---

20  Isaiah 48:9; Ezekiel 20:44; 36:22

21  See Romans 3:26; Hebrews 12:2

22  See Ephesians 5:26

23  See 2 Samuel 22:36; Psalm 18:35; 2 Corinthians 10:1

24  Exodus 34:5-7; Psalm 31:21

He is so quick to forgive. [25]

If we cherish our forgiveness, celebrate our sanctification, and appreciate our justification when all we brought to the courtroom were dirty rags, [26] let us bless our covenantal mother in word and deed, grieve over her sins in prayer, and stand with her wayward sons with support and solidarity till Kingdom Come.

---

25    Exodus 34:5-7; Isaiah 43:25; Colossians 3:13

26    Isaiah 64:6

CHAPTER FOUR

# HE DOES NOT FORGET HER

*"O Israel, you will not be forgotten by Me! I have blotted out, like a thick cloud, your transgressions, and like a cloud, your sins. Return to Me, for I have redeemed you."* [1]

What qualifies something as "worth" praying about? Is there anything we cannot or should not discuss with our Father in Heaven? Does the LORD of Heaven and Earth care about our weather and children and coffee? Or lack thereof?

Of course He does.

Is He so big that He refuses to condescend? No, that god's name is Allah. [2] The God of Israel must eat His ego just to call the stars out to shine every night and He does it anyway. [3] Not once has He complained; instead, He delights in His craftsmanship. [4]

---

1   Isaiah 44:21b-22

2   This conviction serves as a primary Muslim objection to the Incarnation; "God is great" and would therefore never interact with humans on such a degrading level. There are numerous contrasts between Islamic and Judeo-Christian theology, but this is a paramount distinction. See Psalm 113:4-9; Philippians 2:5-11

3   See Psalm 113:4-9

4   See Psalm 8:3-5; Proverbs 8:22-31

Is the God and Father of our LORD Jesus so small He cannot concern Himself with our lives? Of course not. [5]

Yet we wonder if we are dispensable.

We might pray about our lives, but do we get out of bed expecting Him to reveal Himself throughout our day? To intervene in our lives before we go to bed?

Do we share a latent accusation with the children of Jacob that perhaps God has forgotten us? [6] It might not even be that He's "too busy." After all, He is sovereign, is He not?

Perhaps He simply doesn't care.

We would never say this out loud. We'd never sing it at church, because it's generally unhelpful for a corporate context—unless we finish "when I feel forgotten" with something like "I know I'm not."

I've never wondered if God remembers everything. I've only feared He does. But nothing passes His sight, and nothing exceeds the limits of His mind.

Four hundred years separated the last prophetic word from the Incarnate Word; Jacob's children felt forgotten, unseen, and exactly the opposite of an object of determined affection. In the last message delivered before the Messenger of

---

5    See Matthew 6:25-34; 10:29-21; Luke 12:29-34

6    See Isaiah 49:14; Malachi 1:2

the Covenant [7] appeared, Israel's Covenant Maker and Keeper identified latent accusations and unbelief in her heart that crippled her relationship to Him: believing He didn't love her, [8] believing He endorsed wickedness and didn't maintain justice, [9] and believing fidelity to their covenant was a vain waste of time. [10] Consequentially, they despised His name, [11] wearied Him with false accusation, [12] robbed Him, [13] and spoken harshly against Him. [14] Their unbelief had created significant relational strain, yet they hadn't noticed the growing disparity between them.

He did.

We can take our own temperature, figuratively speaking, when we put our heads on our pillows at night. We are the most honest with ourselves when all our buddies are gone, all our songs are silent, all our distractions are quiet, and the lights are off. It is easy to discern what our "pillow top theology" is, even if the results are unflattering, even when our theological temperature is more feverish than we'd like it to be. No one who puts

7   See Isaiah 49:14; Malachi 1:2

8   Malachi 1:2

9   Malachi 2:17

10   Malachi 3:13-14

11   Malachi 1:6

12   Malachi 2:17

13   Malachi 3:8

14   Malachi 3:13

their head on their pillow at night believing God does not love them, isn't worth loving in return (it wouldn't be a return, then, would it?), or that He is not the just God He claims to be has a biblically robust "pillow-top theology," and certainly does not feel *seen* or *significant* to Jesus. You believe lies like that when you feel forgotten.

Israel felt forgotten.

Affliction and trial have their way of pressing us into corners, and Israel is no different. The priest Zechariah felt so forgotten that he couldn't believe Gabriel's words when he heard them.[15] Martha felt forgotten in her grief and couldn't believe God could write His own rules about when and how He could intervene in her life.[16] Zion would hear Isaiah's promises of restoration and sigh in response:

> "The LORD has forsaken me; my Lord has forgotten me."[17]

On paper, it's laughable. There are only so many pages to turn between the promises of Hebron,[18] the parting of the Red Sea,[19] the psalms, and all the prophets. The spectacle of divine intervention! The display of holy attention!

---

15    See Luke 1:7-18

16    See John 11:17-27

17    Isaiah 49:14

18    See Genesis 13:18; 15:1-20

19    Exodus 14:1-31

If Scripture tells us anything, it's that heaven is *constantly* thinking about Israel. [20] The Great King is *constantly* thinking about His holy city. [21] *Constantly.* She is, indeed, the "apple of His eye." [22]

He would hear this accusation, this unbelief, and respond in a way that almost seems incredulous if we don't heed His illustration:

> "Can a woman forget her nursing child,
>
> that she should have no compassion on the son of her womb?
>
> Even these may forget,
>
> yet I will not forget you."
>
> Behold, I have engraved you on the palms of My hands;
>
> your walls are continually before Me." [23]

He sees all her needs and hears all her cries; He knows what she needs to be safe and will ensure she receives them all, down to the last stone she needs to rebuild her walls. [24] "'As I live,' declares the LORD, 'you shall put them all on as an ornament; you shall bind them on as a bride does.'" [25] Jerusalem's security,

---

20   Deuteronomy 32:10; Psalm 17:8; 139:17-18; Isaiah 49:16; Zechariah 2:8

21   Psalm 48:2; Isaiah 49:16; Matthew 5:35

22   Deuteronomy 32:9-11; Zechariah 2:8

23   Isaiah 49:15-16

24   Isaiah 49:17

25   Isaiah 49:18

safety, and stonework are often spoken of by the prophets as wedding attire because *she is His bride.* [26] Jerusalem is not Jesus' hobby; she is His namesake, [27] His wife, [28] and His future home. [29]

She cannot be forgotten.

We are her children, and so He cannot forget us either. [30] Our covenantal security is bound to hers, and thus we can never be forsaken. [31]

When we wonder, and when our trust begins to wane and wander, we can remember Thomas' grief and discouragement after he watched his Rabbi get betrayed, beat up, and brutalized before getting buried in a garden tomb. [32] "I'll believe He's still alive when I see Him walking around with the holes in His hand." [33]

And he did. [34]

Even after the resurrection, Jesus bore—and bears—His scars of execution; His wounds by bloody crucifixion carved this costly covenant

---

26  See Isaiah 54:5,11-12; 61:3,10; Revelation 21:1-2,10-21

27  Psalm 48:2; Daniel 9:19; Matthew 5:35

28  Revelation 21:9-10

29  See Isaiah 24:23; Revelation 21:22

30  Galatians 4:26

31  John 14:18-24

32  John 19:41

33  John 20:24-25

34  John 20:26-29

into His Incarnate flesh. In all the coming millennia of the ages, they'll remind even us that the only names and memories flung into a sea of forgetfulness are our accusers and treasons.

But heaven will always know our names. [35]

---

35    Luke 10:20

CHAPTER FIVE

# HE DELIGHTS IN HER

*"I will recount the steadfast love of the LORD, the praises of the LORD, according to all the LORD has granted us, and the great goodness of the house of Israel that He has granted according to His compassion, according to the abundance of His steadfast love. For He said, 'Surely they are My people, children who will not deal falsely.' And He became their Savior. In all their affliction He was afflicted, and the angel of His presence saved them; in His love and in His pity He redeemed them He lifted them up and carried them all the days of old."* [1]

*"The whole outlook of mankind might be changed if we could all believe that we dwell under a friendly sky and that the God of heaven, though exalted in power and majesty, is eager to be friends with us. But sin has made us timid and self-conscious, as well it might. Years of rebellion against God have bred in us a fear that cannot be overcome in a day. The captured rebel does not enter willingly into the presence of the King he has so long fought unsuccessfully to overthrow."* [2]

Perhaps most difficult for us to believe and receive as truth is the delight of God over our

1   Isaiah 63"7-10

2   Tozer, A.W. (1961). *The Knowledge of the Holy.* New York: HarperCollins, 83-84.

lives. That we could be forgiven, legally, is one idea we may intellectually assent to. That we could be loved, technically, we may believe and buy into. That He would *delight* in us, however, is quite another. I've met few souls who allow their Maker to *enjoy* them. We are not without good reason to stare at His delight with puzzled eyes. It makes sense, then, to be cautious in His presence—but that is not what His blood bought us into. [3] We become His children in Jesus. [4] We become His ambassadors. [5] We become His friends. [6] When we come to Him, we are to come boldly to beg for help He already knows we need and already has prepared. He'll meet us on the way and let us cling to Him on the road home. [7] More than that, He'll toss us on His shoulders and "joyfully carry" [8] us.

Jesus' intercession for us made evident in His commitment to see us through our stupidity is our only hope of a healthy relationship with Him through the ages. We need Him. When we wander, we need Him to come after us. When we lie and deceive and hide and cloak, we need Him to turn the lights on and expose us. We can trust that He will—and when He does, we will

3   1 Corinthians 6:20; 7:23

4   Ephesians 1:2-6; 1 John 3:1

5   2 Corinthians 5:20

6   See John 15:14-15

7   Luke 15:20-22

8   Luke 15:5

discover depths of gentleness enabling Him to expose sin while covering sinners in love. [9] What confidence, though, can we have that we do not just endlessly aggravate Him with our immaturity?

When David was a young man (some time after killing Goliath, years after receiving the prophet's anointing to be king, and not long after marrying the king's daughter and then fleeing his jealous father-in-law's bloodthirsty hand), he lived through a significant season of compromise and moral failure that does not often get airtime in sermons. When we think of "David's sin," we think "Bathsheba." [10] We think "adultery" and "murder." We don't usually think "the-time-he-made-buddies-with-the-enemy-and-lied-to-everyone-for-years-to-survive-and-nearly-got-all-his-friends-killed." But he did. [11] The precious years spent in the hidden quiet of Bethlehem's back hills were long gone. The fame and notoriety as a wise and gifted warrior in the king's courts faded for the shadows of fugitive flight. His marriage to Saul's daughter collapsed. His brotherhood with Saul's son fell casualty to duty and allegiance. The roof over his head was traded for the stars. The walls of his home were that of dank caves instead of palatial interiors. And his confidence in the sustaining hand of God had eroded with fatigue and discouragement.

---

9    Proverbs 10:12; 17:9; James 5:20; 1 Peter 4:8

10    See 2 Samuel 11:1-27

11    See 1 Samuel 27:1-30:6

Then every disillusioned guy in Israel with debt and a record came to join him. [12]

It is a testament to David's leadership skills that even in such a season and with such a battalion of misfit toys under him, he could manipulate the situation to his gain and transform his motley crew into a band of brothers fit for any battle. He wasn't just good at leading; he was good at leading and *lying* about it. And for sixteen months, after years of wilderness wandering and fleeing Saul's headhunters, he based his facade and compromise in Ziklag.

Then one day, he came home and Ziklag was gone. His home was a pile of ash. His buddies' homes were piles of ash. And all their wives and children were gone. Every enemy was onto him. And now all his guys wanted to kill him.

In the rubble of a razed Ziklag and God's intervening hand, David's crutches of self-reliance and self-preservation splintered underneath him. The gig was up. God exposed his compromise, and all his buddies saw him for the fraud he was. No longer were Saul or his mob affiliates his biggest concern, because now "David's mighty men" wanted David dead.

Somehow, David was able to see this moment for the mercy of Jesus that it was, bent his knees, and asked heaven for help. [13]

---

12    1 Samuel 22:2

13    1 Samuel 22:2

*The audacity,* honestly.

Yet heaven responded: "Pursue, for you shall surely overtake [the guys who burned your town and kidnapped your family] and without fail recover all." [14]

So he did.

His friends with heavy stones and loaded guns got their wives and kids back as well, so they decided to not kill David.

Then, through a series of circumstances David had nothing to do with, Saul died. So did all his sons. David began his ascent to the throne of Israel, and the promises of God over his life—the irrevocable, irrefutable promises of God—began to come to pass. [15]

And in the rubble of a razed Ziklag, David sang:

"He delivered me because He delighted in me." [16]

The LORD did not intervene in David's life because David was a man of integrity. No; even as the song continued, David had to trade the facts of his behavior for the truth of how God saw and defined him [17]—which is, truthfully, the only way out of the prison of shame and back on the road of sanctification. David's only righteousness was that imputed to him by the

14   1 Samuel 30:8b, NKJV

15   See 1 Samuel 16:1,13

16   Psalm 18:19, NKJV

17   See Psalm 18:20-30

Righteous One, [18] and he knew it. [19] The LORD intervened in David's life simply because He delighted in David.

Why would He delight in a manipulative liar?

Let us turn to the City destined to be called "THE LORD OUR RIGHTEOUSNESS;" [20] for in her story is our story. In her is David's story, and from her will reign David's Son.

> "Whereas you have been forsaken and hated, I will make you majestic forever, from age to age...you shall know that I, the LORD, am your Savior and your Redeemer, the Mighty One of Jacob." [21]

In Jesus' early months of ministry, He returned to a synagogue He often attended, "as was His habit," [22] and on a particular day someone handed Him the scroll of Isaiah's prophecies, written seven centuries before His birth in Bethlehem. [23] He opened it to the start of what we now call "chapter sixty-one," and read thus:

> "The Spirit of the LORD is upon Me,
>
> because He has anointed Me
>
> to proclaim good news to the poor.

---

18    Psalm 50:1; Isaiah 63:1; 1 John 2:1

19    See Psalm 18:24

20    Jeremiah 23:55; 33:16

21    See Isaiah 60:15-16

22    Luke 4:16, NKJV

23    See Micah 5:2; Matthew 2:1,5-6; John 7:42

He has sent Me to proclaim liberty to the captives and recovering of sight to the blind,

to set at liberty those who are oppressed,

to proclaim the year of the LORD's favor." [24]

Then He looked around at those listening and told them, "Today this Scripture has been fulfilled in your hearing." [25]

Isaiah didn't put a full stop after "favor." There's more to the passage that Jesus *didn't* fulfill that day, which means there are still yet words in this prophecy upon which we hang our hopes. Here is Isaiah's original verse:

"The Spirit of the LORD God is upon Me,

because the LORD has anointed Me

to bring good news to the poor;

He has sent Me to bind up the brokenhearted,

to proclaim the year of the LORD's favor,

and the Day of vengeance of our God;

to comfort all who mourn;

to grant those who mourn in Zion—

to give them a beautiful headdress instead of ashes, the oil of gladness instead of mourning,

the garment of praise instead of a faint

---

24  Isaiah 61:1-2a

25  Luke 4:21

spirit;

that they may be called oaks of
righteousness,

the planting of the LORD,
that He may be glorified." [26]

It is easy to see, even grammatically, these three
verses are one continuous thought. Why did
Jesus stop just before "the Day of vengeance"?

Because it wasn't the Day of Vengeance yet.

What is the "Day of Vengeance"?

The prophetic texts are laced with the coming
Day of the LORD, when the Son of David—the
Psalm 2 "anointed of the LORD" [27]—receives
the throne covenantally promised to Him by
His Father [28] and anticipated throughout the
patriarchs, prophets, and psalmists as the Seed
promised to defeat the devil in Genesis three. [29]
The "Day of Vengeance" described by Isaiah
is the "Day of the LORD," when He settles the
"controversy of Zion." [30] The detailed promises
of this coming Day are as beautiful as they are
vast. She (Jerusalem) will be safe from all her

---

26    Isaiah 61:1-3

27    See Psalm 2:6

28    See 2 Samuel 7

29    See Genesis 3:15

30    See Proverbs 16:4; Isaiah 2:12-17; 34:8; 61:2; Joel 2:31; Zechariah 14:1

aggressors. [31] She will "lay down safely." [32] The nations will stream to her. [33] She will be established, never to be moved. [34] All her children will know the LORD. [35] *All*. Evangelism will dry up the moment He appears. "'Then you shall know Me,' says the LORD." [36] She has no greater hope but Him. She has no other hope *besides* Him. Nor do we: it is in this "great and terrible" [37] Day that will see the consummation of all prophecy, the end of all transgression, the resurrection of the saints, and a myriad of other promises we're still waiting on. [38]

"For I the LORD love justice," He says as He explains this year of favor and Day of vengeance, "and I will make an everlasting covenant with them." [39] The deliverance of Zion is because of the Everlasting Covenant; truly there is no Everlasting Covenant without her. He authored it that way. So her deliverance is important to us because our deliverance hinges on hers.

---

31    Isaiah 49:23; Zechariah 12:9; 14:3

32    Jeremiah 33:16; Zechariah 14:11

33    Isaiah 55:5; 60:3-5; Jeremiah 3:17; Micah 4:2; Zechariah 8:22; Revelation 21:24

34    Psalm 46:5

35    See Isaiah 54:13; Jeremiah 30:10; 31:34; John 6:45

36    Isaiah 49:23; Jeremiah 31:34; Ezekiel 20:38

37    Joel 2:11

38    See Daniel 9:24, though the prophetic literature is laced with language of the likes of a restoration we've not yet seen

39    Isaiah 61:8

Either He is true to His Word and keeps His covenant, or He doesn't. Either Jerusalem will be kept from abandonment, or she won't. And our fate is her fate.

Fortunately, Scripture is clear: He will not abandon Jerusalem.[40]

Not because she earned His faithfulness.

Not because she kept the covenant.

Not because she preserved her own fidelity.

Because *He loves justice*.

Because He loves *her*.

"Justice" here means His city knows and loves Him. He will orchestrate history and pursue her heart until she does. Like David, He will confront her compromise and lay low her lies until in the ashes of Ziklag, she lifts her eyes to see her King standing over all her enemies—including and especially herself—when the "new song" she erupted at His resurrection returns to her walls after having covered the globe.[41] There has always been international intention to the Everlasting Covenant; it was made with Jerusalem, it spread from Jerusalem, and it will return to Jerusalem. It is hers to have and hold. It is *her* hope. It is *her* calling and destiny. We are but grafted into it. Isaiah continues: "For

---

40   Jeremiah 31:35-37

41   See Isaiah 24:14-16; 42:10-14; Matthew 23:37-39; 24:14; Acts 1:6-8

Zion's sake I will not keep silent,"[42] as "for a long time I have held My peace; I have kept still and restrained Myself; now I will cry out like a woman in labor; I will gasp and pant."[43]

"Shall I bring to the point of birth and not cause to bring forth?"[44] Of course not. The LORD will deliver, even when it looks like trouble to such a degree men will double over in pain.[45] Even then, He will bring His promises to pass. Even then, the New Song will return to the city it erupted from and in the darkest hour of blasphemy, sin, compromise, and antichristic refrains, her slaughtered firstborn will come to her and she will sing, "Blessed is He!"[46] Indeed, blessed is He who comes in the name of the LORD. Blessed is He who keeps His covenant; blessed is He who keeps His Word. When her sin catches up to her and her enemies surround and raze her for the last time, the Son of David will stand again on the Mount of Olives and the City of David will sing from her rubble: "Blessed is He who delivered me because He delights in me."[47]

In that Day:

"You shall no more be termed Forsaken,

---

42  Isaiah 62:1

43  Isaiah 42:14

44  Isaiah 66:9

45  Jeremiah 30:5-7

46  See Psalm 118:26; Zechariah 12:10; Matthew 23:37-39

47  Psalm 18:19

and your land shall no more be termed Desolate, but you shall be called My Delight Is In Her,

and your land Married,

for the LORD delights in you,

and your land shall be Married.

For as a young man marries a young woman,

so shall your sons marry you,

and as the bridegroom rejoices over the bride,

so shall your God rejoice over you." [48]

Most precious of this truth, the truth that no matter what He delights in her, is Zephaniah's succinct prophecy: When Jerusalem is at her most rebellious, defiled, and dirtiest, [49] when she trusts in everything but Jesus, [50] when He hedges her in with thorns and nations, when He gathers her enemies against her so He can offend with His elective grace and vindicate His harlot wife, [51] when He uses her redemption to save the nations and cover the earth with the knowledge of the glory of God, [52] when He meets her darkest shame to magnify His deepest

48    Isaiah 62:4-5

49    Zephaniah 3:1

50    Jeremiah 9:23-24; Zephaniah 3:2; 1 Corinthians 1:31; 2 Corinthians 10:17

51    Hosea 1:1-3; 3:1; Zephaniah 3:8

52    Zephaniah 3:9; Habakkuk 2:14; 2 Corinthians 4:6

grace, [53] when He draws her to Himself with His light burden and easy yoke, [54] when He purges her of deceit and instills in her unflinching declarations of truth, [55] when He eleventh-hour saves her from her enemies (however well deserved), when He stands in the midst of her such that she will not be moved and erases her guilt, shuts the mouth of her accuser, and smashes the head of Eden's serpent, [56] "on that day it shall be said to Jerusalem:

'Fear not, O Zion;

let not your hands grow weak. [57]

The LORD your God is in your midst,

a mighty one [58] who will save;

He will rejoice over you with gladness;

He will quiet you with His love;

He will exult over you with loud singing.

I will gather those of you who mourn for the festival,

so that you will no longer suffer reproach.

Behold, at that time I will deal

---

53    Isaiah 54:4; Zephaniah 3:11

54    Zephaniah 3:12; Matthew 11:28-30

55    Zephaniah 3:13

56    Genesis 3:15; Psalm 46:1-11; Zephaniah 3:14-15; Zechariah 14:3-9

57    See also Isaiah 35:3

58    Psalm 45:3; 50:1; 132:3,5; Isaiah 1:24; 20:34

with all your oppressors.

And I will save the lame

and gather the outcast,

and I will change their shame into praise

and renown in all the earth.

At that time I will gather you in,

at the time when I gather you together;

for I will make you renowned and praised

among all the peoples of the earth,

When I restore your fortunes before your eyes," says the LORD. [59]

In the ashes of Jerusalem's Ziklag, the ransomed daughters of David won't be the only ones with a song of deliverance. Her Husband will erupt with a melody of His very own.

The whole world will hear it.

---

59    Zephaniah 3:16-20

CHAPTER SIX

# HE DISCIPLINES HER

*"If the LORD of hosts had not left us a few survivors, we would have been like Sodom, and become like Gomorrah."*[1]

It is not difficult to find reasons to demerit Jerusalem; not through history, and certainly not today. She has never been without guilt or bloodstain, and despite the juggernaut of anti-Semitic propaganda through the centuries, no one *needs* to fabricate accusations against her. We don't need to point her sins and stains out to the Judge—He is painfully and thoroughly aware of them all. [2] It is not happenstance that judgment will begin with her, but we cannot forget salvation begins with her as well. [3] As much as we rely on the justice of the Judge of the ages letting no injustice past His gavel, we must also see the "apple of [His own] eye" [4] through lenses colored by the same saving grace we beg for ourselves, and have access to only

1    Isaiah 1:9; cf Romans 9:29

2    See Psalm 139; Proverbs 5:21-23; 15:3; Hebrews 4:13. The LORD is omniscient. He sees and knows all. He is all too familiar with the record of Israel's wrongs, and is committed to see them through to the end (see Jeremiah 31:31-37).

3    Romans 1:16; 2:2-11

4    Deuteronomy 32:10; Zechariah 2:8

through the covenant He initiated with her to begin with. [5]

Israel is identified as God's "firstborn."[6] As a child, Israel has a father. This is a simplistic but important point: Jacob is not a bastard. Someone is taking responsibility for his growth and development, and not out of pity: Jacob bears his Father's blood and name.

His Father is very committed to him. [7]

In Luke 19, Jesus took responsibility for the war and destruction that would come to Jerusalem just a few decades later—and identified the events of AD 70 as a disciplinary consequence to their rejection of Him when He visited them. [8] This disobedience cost Jacob, and it grieved his Father. But it was not the end of Jacob's story or sonship.

Our hope and vision for our own eternal sanctification and training is anchored in Jesus' commitment to us being stronger than our commitment to Him. [9] It cannot be up to us to keep ourselves from wandering, stumbling, or failing. It is up to Him, His hand, and His Spirit. It is on us to yield, to be sure, and He will discipline us when we don't *because He*

---

5   See Jeremiah 31:31-37; Romans 9:3-5; Ephesians 2:11-22

6   Exodus 4:22; Jeremiah 31:9

7   See Jeremiah 31:20,31-37

8   See Luke 19:41-44

9   See 1 Corinthians 1:8; Philippians 1:6

*cares.* Any good parent would, and He is a better parent than we'll ever be. [10] The psalmist made clear heaven's heart and highest vision for our lives is not that we would just be bound and tethered to a task, but that we'd know His voice [11] and follow Him [12] without requiring a bit and bridle to break us in as though we were stubborn stallions. [13]

So it was with David, so it was with Jesus; [14] so it is with us, [15] because it is with Jacob.

The prophetic texts all point towards the coming "Day of the LORD," which is identified as the end of this era of redemptive and eternal history and the start of the next age. Perhaps the most beautiful element of this coming Day, second to the manifest presence of the One we love and confess, [16] is the end of iniquity. [17] His appearing will commence our final freedom from our own treason. With all the LORD is taking it

---

10   See Psalm 27:10; Matthew 6:9-11

11   See Psalm 95:7; John 10:3-4,16,27

12   See Matthew 10:38

13   See Psalm 32:8-9

14   Hebrews 5:8; 12:1-11

15   Isaiah 55:3

16   Isaiah 24:23; Revelation 21:22-23

17   The Day of the LORD and appearance of the Son of Man in the clouds (Daniel 7:13-14) will bring about the end of iniquity (Daniel 9:24), but sin and deception will not meet its final end until the end of Jesus' 1,000-year reign (Revelation 20:2-3).

upon Himself to avenge, [18] His unwavering commitment to absolute and total justice, [19] and what it cost Him to secure forgiveness and redemption, [20] it should come as no surprise to us when the prophets and psalmists employ language of severity [21] to describe what this final purge of wickedness from the earth will look like.

It should also not surprise us that Jacob will be at the center of the storm. [22]

What Daniel called (and Jesus quoted as) the "great tribulation," Jeremiah referred to as the "time of Jacob's trouble."[23] All the prophets who described this time—Jesus included—identified it as characterized by unprecedented suffering. It feels impossible when we scour the texts and read of its scale; we can jog through the Rolodex records in our minds of events through history, even recently in our grandparents' generation or our own now, with wide and worried eyes: the Holocaust was bad. The Syrian Civil War is bad. Scripture says this final time of trouble—Jacob's trouble—will be worse? That's rightly horrifying.

18    See Deuteronomy 32:35,41,43; Isaiah 34:8; 61:2; 63:4; Jeremiah 11:20; Romans 12:19; 1 Thessalonians 4:6

19    Deuteronomy 16:19; 24:17-19; Job 8:3; 34:12; 37:23; Psalm 10:18; 33:5; 37:28; 89:14; Isaiah 1:27; 42:3; 51:4; 61:8

20    1 Corinthians 6:20

21    See Jeremiah 23:20; 30:7; Daniel 9:24-27; 12:1,7; Zechariah 14:1-2; Matthew 24:21-22; Mark 13:19-20

22    Zechariah 12:2-3

23    Jeremiah 30:7; Daniel 12:1; Matthew 24:21

Why the severity?

Why would He be willing to do this?

"Train a child in the way he should go, and when he is old he will not depart from it." [24] If this is true for us as broken humans and fallible parents, it surely is true for the Father of lights and glory. He has an end in mind for wayward Jacob, and it is redemptive, beautiful, and glorious. Jacob cannot *earn* his place or position at his Father's table, but he must be *trustworthy* with it. If Jesus had to "learn obedience by what He suffered," [25] so will Jacob, and so will we. The discipline of heaven is not arbitrary or abusive; in fact, much of what we suffer in this age is for sake of shaping us for the next. The only distinction between our learning curve and Jesus' is that we *deserve* punishment for stupid decisions and He did and does not; however, our Father is not out to *punish* us. He is a Potter *shaping* us. Not all suffering is the result of something we "deserve." [26] In fact, it is often offensive because we have good reason to believe we *don't*. [27]

Jacob's sons will have significant positions of authority under the reign of King Jesus—because He appointed them to these positions; certainly not because they deserved or earned them. Much

24  Proverbs 22:6

25  Hebrews 5:8

26  See Hebrews 12:1-11

27  Job 27:2

like tax collectors and thieves called to follow Him, so these twenty-four sons were chosen by the Sovereign. Ages from now, Judah nor Reuben nor Peter nor Thomas will be defined by the dumb things they said and did in this age—and *thank God,* neither will we. Paul put it this way:

> "Therefore, since we have been justified by faith, we have peace with God through our Lord Jesus Christ. Through Him we have also obtained access by faith into this grace in which we stand, and we rejoice in hope of the glory of God. Not only that, but we rejoice in our sufferings, knowing that suffering produces endurance, and endurance produces character, and character produces hope, and hope does not put us to shame, because God's love has been poured into our hearts through the Holy Spirit who has been given to us." [28]

Our responsibility in this age is to keep perspective of the next; it is only in light of eternity that we can trust Jesus to make amends for all the wrongs we commit, and deal appropriately with those committed against us. What we *cannot* do is take it upon ourselves to discipline His children as though we are their parent; no, we are their peers, fellow siblings and fellow heirs. [29] We must cling to grace for ourselves and our brothers and sisters, and when they wander we must refuse

---

28    Romans 5:1-5

29    Ephesians 3:6

the murderous apathy of Cain; [30] we have to be the brother who keeps the other, and in this way we are not to point to Jacob's rebellion. We cannot be the haughty brother who refuses to celebrate the prodigal's homecoming—why go to bed drunk on our own ego when we can be drunk on our Father's wine? [31]

Like Jeremiah, let us stand *against* Jacob's sin but *for* him in intercession and solidarity, reminding him who he is and all he is meant to become.

---

30    See Genesis 4:3-10

31    See Luke 15:11-32; Ephesians 5:18

CHAPTER SEVEN

# HE REBUILDS HER

*"O afflicted one, storm-tossed and not comforted, behold, I will set your stones in antimony, and lay your foundations with sapphires.* [1]

*Lord, help us to wonder at the beauty in the mystery; help us to handle it rightly, to lose ourselves to the tides in the oceans of Your goodness. Give us sight for eternity. Give us the heart and hands of advocacy. Put in us something of what You put in Nehemiah—conviction for Your bride's destiny, and camaraderie to bring her into it.*

Jesus is a brilliant Architect, and Abraham's dream of the Eternal City built by God [2] is still the yearning of this age. It is still the inheritance of the saints. [3] "To Him who can do exceedingly and abundantly beyond anything we can ask or think" [4] we can assign no limitations. When He says He will restore all things, [5] He will *restore all*

---

1   Isaiah 54:11

2   Hebrews 11:10

3   Colossians 1:12

4   Ephesians 3:20-21

5   See Revelation 21:1-4

*things.* He'll restore the years lost to rebellion.[6] He'll restore the harvest devoured by locusts.[7] He'll restore the inheritance squandered by our drunken stupor.[8]

And He'll restore the Kingdom to Israel.[9]

Why is this important? Because the "blessing" destined for "every nation" to come "through" Israel hinges upon it.[10] The integrity of the Word of God—the issue under assault since Eden—is bankrupt without it.[11] The eternal and international intention to the Everlasting Covenant is knit to the welfare and well-being of Jerusalem. We'll spend the next age in tangible proximity to Jesus because He'll be *in* Jerusalem.[12] Are the promises of Scripture metaphorical? Only insofar as we can apply the revelation of God's personality as revealed in the tangible actions described by the psalmists, prophets, and apostles to our daily lives. Meaning we *glean* from the texts truths of Jesus' nature and character and we *rely* on the fact that He'll keep His word. His interaction with humanity has always had geographic implications. This

---

6    Jeremiah 31:18-20

7    Joel 2:25

8    See Luke 15:11-32

9    Acts 1:6-8

10    Genesis 22:18

11    See Genesis 3:1

12    Isaiah 24:23; Revelation 21:22-23

is His earth; [13] He made it, and He made it "good."[14] He's going to make it even better.[15]

What happens after the discipline and decimation of Jacob's trouble? The revelation of the glory of God according to "all the good I will do to [her]."[16] Jesus isn't intimidated by any obstacle hell or humans can put in His way, and He is so committed to the long game. A seed was conceived in the promises of Eden, [17] and its fruition will display the intervening and sovereign hand of God to a mightier and more wonderful degree than even the deliverance of a nation through the Red Sea. [18]

"Shall I bring to the time of birth, and not cause delivery?" asks He who forms us in the womb.[19] "Shall *I who cause delivery* shut up the womb?"[20] Is there a balm in Gilead?[21] Scripture poses rhetorical questions to us only for the Spirit who helps us to come to our shoulders and whisper in our ears the obvious answers: *He finishes what He starts. Of course there is*

13   Psalm 24:1; 1 Corinthians 10:26-28

14   Genesis 1:10, 25, 31

15   Revelation 21:1

16   Jeremiah 32:40,42

17   See Genesis 3:15

18   See Jeremiah 16:14-15; 23:5-8; Micah 7:15

19   Isaiah 66:9a

20   Isaiah 66:9b, emphasis added

21   See Jeremiah 8:22

*a balm in Gilead.* So "rejoice with Jerusalem, all you who love her; rejoice for joy with her, all you who mourn for her, that you may feed and be satisfied with the consolation of her bosom, that you may drink deeply and be delighted with the abundance of her glory."[22] Come, you children of Zion,[23] and get in on your mother's abundance. Drinks are on the house.[24]

There's a beautiful, nuanced use of the term "multicolored" by the apostles. Paul identified the purpose to this age and the mystery of Christ crucified as this: the revelation of the "manifold," or multicolored wisdom of God *through* the Church *to* the powers and principalities of the air.[25] "Multicolored" like the prismatic display of color bouncing off a diamond in shining light. James used the same word to describe our trials and tribulations—the "various kinds"[26] we find ourselves in. "Various" and "manifold" each respectively mean, more literally, multicolored. In both cases, it is knit to the point and purpose of suffering in our lives.

John gives us a portrait of God's use of these trials, and his prophecy is built upon Isaiah's. The spirit of prophecy is the testimony of Jesus,[27]

---

22    Isaiah 66:10-11

23    Galatians 4:22-31

24    Isaiah 55:1

25    Ephesians 3:10

26    James 1:2

27    Revelation 19:10

so we are here leaning on and gleaning from who Jesus is and what He does and is doing as revealed and described in these texts; paramount to our discipleship, obedience, and love for Him in this age is understanding His promises and purposes to the suffering we endure, and endure we must.

Again, Jerusalem serves us with our object lesson: "O you afflicted, tossed with tempest and not comforted," [28] He says to her.

> "Behold, I will lay your stones *with colorful gems,* and lay your foundations with sapphires. I will make your pinnacles of rubies, your gates of crystal, and all your walls of precious stones." [29]

Meaning: *Jerusalem, I'm going to redeem all your suffering and use every trial and wound to rebuild you. I'm going to beautify your pain, and by it fortify you.*

These are beautiful promises, but let's not insult them by relegating them to ethereal simplicity. *He really is going to rebuild Jerusalem,* and this is the hope all the prophets, apostles, and people of old hung their faith on. This is the city Abraham looked and waited for. This is the promise David's covenant is built on, and it's what the boys clung to on the Mount of Olives when they asked their King when He'd take His throne. When He'd finished what He's started.

---

28    Isaiah 54:11a, NKJV

29    Isaiah 54:11b-12, NKJV, emphasis added.

John elaborates, having seen this City coming down from heaven "having the glory of God, its radiance like a most rare jewel, like a jasper, clear as crystal. It had a great, high wall, with twelve gates, and at the gates twelve angels, and on the gates the names of the twelve tribes of Israel were inscribed….the foundations of the wall of the city were adorned with every kind of jewel. The first was jasper, the second sapphire, the third agate, the fourth emerald, the fifth onyx, the sixth carnelian, the seventh chrysolite, the eighth beryl, the ninth topaz, the tenth chrysoprase, the eleventh jacinth, the twelfth amethyst." [30] The gates are cut from a single pearl each, and the streets of the city are "pure gold, like transparent glass." [31]

Anchoring both the prophet and the apostle's steadfast hope of restoration is the destruction it comes on the heels of. "In overflowing anger for a moment I hid My face from you," and the sting of rejection felt to her a bit like a young woman turned away by her husband [32] in the early days and weeks of marriage. It is by His preserving power she seeks Him still, even if only by zeal without knowledge, [33] and the same preserving power that will keep her through the multicolored trouble and trial until He returns,

---

30    Revelation 21:11-12,19-20

31    Revelation 21:21

32    See Isaiah 54:6-8

33    See Romans 10:1-3

when "all [her] children will be taught by the LORD." [34]

It is the same power that preserves us. [35]

The same power that pulled Jesus out of the grave. [36]

The same power that vindicates His saints and delivers our inheritance as promised. [37]

The same power that restores a broken fisherman on the brink of blasphemy. [38]

In Jerusalem is a type of Peter, by whose early confession the foundation of the faith was built; by her patriarchs and prophets and promises and laws the ground was cleared for the Gospel foundation to be laid. [39] "On this rock I will build My *ecclesia*," [40] said the Son of David. Peter, Cephas, was a man of promise. Jesus pulled him from obscurity and handed him a future he couldn't earn and didn't deserve; gave him opportunities the rest of society had denied him, and trained him for eternally significant leadership. And then when trouble came, all his rhetoric dissipated like the embers of the

---

34   Isaiah 54:13

35   Ephesians 1:13-14

36   Ephesians 1:19-20

37   Isaiah 54:17

38   See Matthew 10:33; 16:22-24; 26:69-75

39   Romans 15:20; 1 Corinthians 3:11; Ephesians 2:20

40   Matthew 16:18; "ecclesia" meaning the Body of Messiah

fire he sat before: "I'll go anywhere! I'll give everything! I'll die with You!"

"No, you won't. [41]

But you will." [42]

This man who denied the Messiah so many times met him later on the shore, only to have the Holy One Incarnate make him breakfast and take him for a walk. Indeed, "[His] gentleness make[s us] great," [43] and His gentleness restored the son of Jonah who'd blown everything. When Jerusalem's covenantal infidelity catches up to her, when she denies Him some too many times before the fire, when she drowns in the rage of the nations she gave herself away to, He will meet her on the shores of restoration, melt her fears, and wash her accusations with one simple question:

"Do you love Me?" [44]

And a bruised, battered, and costly-restored Zion will finally begin to sing. [45]

41   Matthew 26:34; John 13:38

42   John 21:18-19

43   2 Samuel 22:36; Psalm 18:35

44   John 21:15-19

45   See Isaiah 12:1-6; 54:1; Zephaniah 3:14-15; Zechariah 9:9

CONCLUSION

# WEIGHING WHAT WE HEAR

If what we believe about God is the most important thing about us, what we believe about Jerusalem is the most important thing we believe about Jesus. What we believe about Jesus makes or breaks our health and vitality until we meet Him in the air. [1]

The narrow road of truth is lined by ditches of "this-sounds-okay, right?" falsehood on either side. On one side is a theological tradition nearly as old as the New Testament; its age criminally lends it credibility, but we seem to skip past the apostle Paul's words explicitly refuting and warning against it. [2] It is now often referred to as "fulfillment," "replacement," or (most audaciously) "covenant" theology, with a kind of evangelical popularity that makes it seem as though there are no other alternatives. This system of thought has had centuries to polish its case for why no promises of God stand particularly for Israel or Jerusalem specifically. It rises and falls on these premises: The people no longer matter. The land no longer matters. The city no longer matters. There's nothing

---

1   John 15:4; 1 Thessalonians 4:16

2   Romans 11:25

unique or particular about ethnic, national, or territorial Israel specifically. All the promises of old were "fulfilled" and summed up in Jesus. It paves a broad and accessible road for hyper-spiritualized doctrine that castrates the promises to the patriarchs, mutes the proclamations of the prophets, bastardizes the Gospel of the Kingdom, and gives terrifying permission for missional apathy. More than anything, it makes Jesus into a manipulative and scheming liar. This has enough airtime on its own, so I'm not going to give place to it here. There's no reason for it to have gained the traction that it did and has, when Paul refuted it so specifically to the Romans. He saw the emerging undercurrents of covenantal animosity and familial insecurity arising in Gentile-majority fellowships with no background in the historic revelation of God given specifically to Jacob's children.

> "I do not want you to be ignorant of this mystery, family, because I don't want intoxicating ignorance to develop into drunken arrogance. I don't want you drunk on your own Gentile ego, because this grace thing can go to your heads." [3]

I worry we didn't listen. [4]

On the other side of the narrow road is a similarly slippery slope into a delusional ditch dug out of

---

3    This is my paraphrase of Romans 11:25

4    For more on this troubled history and its devastating consequences, watch *Covenant and Controversy Part I: The Great Rage* for free at covenant-andcontroversy.com/films

a different kind of Gospel ignorance. Evangelical dispensationalism and its disposition to "dual-covenant" theology proposes such asinine conclusions Charles Spurgeon could only shake his head when he heard it: "We never know what we shall hear next, and perhaps it is a mercy that these absurdities are revealed at one time, in order that we may be able to endure their stupidity without dying of amazement." [5]

The popularity of these ditches only betrays our biblical illiteracy. We have no excuse. We have the Word. We have the Holy Spirit. We have everything we need. [6] We can no longer treat the issue and theology of Israel and Jerusalem as a hobby for YouTube theologians and date-setting end-time "preppers." If we love Jesus, we love His appearing. If we love His name, we care about the integrity of His Word.

It's very simple.

If we love the Great King, we necessarily love His city as well.

*"Pray for the peace of Jerusalem."*[7]

---

5    Spurgeon, C.H. *Jesus Christ Immutable*. Metropolitan Tabernacle Pulpit, 56 Volumes. (London: Passmore and Alabaster, 1862–1917; reprint Pasadena, Texas: Pilgrim Publications, 1973), 15:8.

6    1 Timothy 2:2

7    Psalm 122:6

APPENDIX A

# CONTENTION AND

# COMPLEXITY

## THE DANGERS OF ZIONISM (AND LACK THEREOF)

*This article first appeared in*
*the* Covenant and Controversy
*online library,* [1] *October 2016*

In late November 1947, the United Nations drafted Resolution 181 as a proposition to partition what had been British Mandate Palestine. Days later, the General Assembly voted by majority to accept the resolution. The Jewish state was but months away from reemerging on the geopolitical stage, and Jerusalem once again poised to confront the nations with "the controversy of Zion." [2] Decades have passed, and Resolution 181 is no longer the only resolution the UN has lodged regarding Israel—but it is one of the few resolutions not serving as condemnations.

---

1   Visit covenantandcontroversy.com for more

2   Isaiah 34:8

For nearly seventy years, the world has been forced to grapple with the legitimacy of the modern state of Israel. Wars and threats of wars have nearly suffocated her. Politicians and theologians alike have drawn their swords for or against her supporters. The movement known as "Zionism," birthed in the late nineteenth century, has driven an effective wedge into global culture, dividing Western and Arab nations alike.

As with any divisive issue, the rage thrives on two sides: those who argue against the legitimacy of the modern State and those who support the State, often unequivocally. The argument has risen to so many decibels, it seems everyone stopped listening to each other a long time ago. "Never Again" has become the mantra of the modern Jewish generation, while accusations of "apartheid" and "occupation" have drowned out the cheers that erupted out of liberated camps upon the Allied arrival as the Second World War came to a close. The two political positions now in question both share a heritage in bankrupt theological foundations and bear toxic theological, ecclesiological and sociological fruit. With mudslinging on all sides, we believe it crucial to think critically and respond biblically to what is fundamentally a Gospel issue.

## THE DANGERS OF ANTI-ZIONISM

As the crucified and risen Jewish King was proclaimed beyond Jerusalem and His precious name reached Rome, the growing Gentile-majority fellowship in this ancient city was admonished by the still-living apostle Saul of Tarsus to "not be ignorant" concerning the mystery of Israel's place in God's cosmic purposes, despite (and in light of!) her rejection of Yeshua and her corporate unbelief post-Golgotha. [3]

We worry Rome didn't listen. Far from a modern invention, the theological foundations for anti-Zionism are nothing new. The theological system almost consistently bleeds into politics since the emergence of the State (though the political position can and does well stand on its own). The system known as "supersessionism," "replacement," "fulfillment," and—most audaciously—"covenant" theology is best described as a system of divestment, built upon a hermeneutic in which all of the covenantal blessings given to the houses of Israel and Judah are "transferred" [4] (read: divested from) to the mostly Gentile Church. To stay faithful to its self-devised hermeneutic, "covenantal theology" must necessarily redefine "covenant," thus marring the very name and nature of the God who makes and keeps said covenant.

---

3   Romans 11:25

4   This word, and its synonyms, is not uncommon amongst divestment theologians. NT Wright uses this word in *The Climax of the Covenant* [(Minneapolis: Fortress Press October 1, 1993), 25.] to say: "[Paul] has systematically transferred the privileges and attributes of 'Israel' to the Messiah and His [new] people [the Church]. It is therefore greatly preferable to take... 'Israel' as a typically Pauline polemical redefinition..."

Moreover, because divestment theology castrates the integrity of covenant, a bankrupt eschatology must necessarily follow. The consequences of this often include selling this unregenerate earth as already renewed, or identifying the prophesied millennial reign of the Messiah as "figurative," with all the improvements laid upon the Church as her responsibility (never mind that it goes without saying, unresurrected corpses cannot resurrect created order). With the covenantal purposes of God skewed and His commitment to make all wrong things right effectively robbed of potency, it follows that our ability to understand the Man Christ Jesus as He has revealed Himself is irreparably compromised.

With these tenets in place, those who hold to divestment ideology (it can hardly be called a theology, such being a knowledge of God), have nothing in place to resist opposition to the modern, supposedly irrelevant, State of Israel. Because the "irrevocable" [5] election of Israel is compromised, mocked and redefined, so is grace. The political anti-Zionism of theological anti-Judaism has a long and sordid history, which has never once produced good fruit. [6]

---

5   Romans 11:29

6   See *Our Hands are Stained with Blood* by Dr. Michael L. Brown, *Lethal Obsession: Anti-Semitism from antiquity to the Global Jihad* by Robert S. Wistrich, *Future Israel: Why Christian anti-Judaism Must be Challenged* by Barry Horner, *Semites and anti-Semites* by Bernard Lewis. Where and when theological philo-Semitism is allowed to flourish there is health to the group that produces it. Likewise, there is death where the inverse is true.

Our very simple litmus test is this: Judge a tree by its fruit. [7]

## THE DANGERS OF ZIONISM

In the latter years of the nineteenth century, theologians began re-evaluating the long-standing tradition that the Church had "superseded" Israel in her covenantal standing as a nation, land and people elected by God. As they formed new conclusions, some swung the pendulum equally too far in the opposite direction; in a manner equally destructive to divestment of Israel's covenantal peculiarity, she was then elevated beyond moral discretion and, sometimes, beyond the need for Calvary. [8] Irishman John Nelson Darby's new theological system was transplanted to America by Charles Scofield and widely popularized by the latter's study Bible. That which we know as "dispensationalism" was born, and not without its consequences.

Darby's construct brings division where Christ brought unity, [9] supposing not one kingdom, but two; not one salvific covenant, but two. Though dispensationalism affirms the future fulfillment of all prophecies and promises to the national, ethnic and geographic Israel, it also

---

7   See Matthew 7:15-20; 12:33; Luke 6:44

8   "I believe that every Jewish person who lives in the light of the Torah, which is the word of God, has a relationship with God and will come to redemption....In fact, trying to convert Jews is a waste of time. Jews already have a covenant with God and that has never been replaced by Christianity." John Hagee in the *Houston Chronicle*, 30 April 1988 (6) 1.

9   See Ephesians 2:14-18

advocates a pre-tribulation rapture, accusing Israel's Shepherd of removing His witness from the earth just before Jacob enters his "time of trouble."[10] Consequently, the emphasis upon Israel as God's "chosen"[11] divorced from any prophetic foresight breeds unbiblical nationalism and conceives naïve political support—which is particularly troublesome with the modern Palestinian controversy. Though both parties involved in the conflict have filthy hands, too many evangelicals (typically American) excuse or overlook any of Israel's legitimate transgressions and funnel huge amounts of money to the Israeli government—not believers in the land, but to the secular political institution. Perhaps most injurious, however, is its logical deductive end: the ideological abortion of missional efforts to bring the "Gospel of the Kingdom" back to wayward Jacob.[12]

## WHY THIS IS A GOSPEL ISSUE

If the arguments and mud swirling and slinging around Jerusalem were simply about soil—dirt— or a geopolitical tension in the Middle East along with every other war and fractured boundary line in the bleeding Arab world, we'd leave it well alone.

---

10    Jeremiah 30:7

11    Deuteronomy 7:6; 14:2; 1 Kings 3:8

12    Matthew 24:14; see also Romans 1:16

If the consequences of these ideologies hadn't historically resulted in genocide and political partnership with a pagan nation, we'd leave it well alone.

If the Judeo-Christian Scriptures were silent on the future of this people, land, nation and city, we'd leave it well alone.

Trouble is, Jerusalem is not just any city. She is "the city of the Great King." [13]

Trouble is, Luther was never quite rebuked for spouting anti-Semitic and anti-Judaic rubbish. Hitler quoted him centuries later to gain Germany's support for the "Final Solution" to the "Jewish question." [14]

Trouble is, the modern State isn't the fruition of Abraham's holy dream. [15]

Trouble is, all of the prophets, all of the apostles and Jesus Himself looked to the Day when Jerusalem would be "established, far from oppression," "majestic forever, a joy from age to age," "a crown of glory in the hand of the LORD," shining with "salvation as a lamp that burns" which all "Gentiles shall see." [16]

---

13  See Psalm 48:2; Matthew 5:35

14  United States Holocaust Memorial Museum. Final Solution. http://www.ushmm.org/wlc/en/article.php?ModuleId=10007328. Accessed 23 July 2015.

15  See Genesis 15:12-21

16  Isaiah 54:14; 60:15; 62:1-3

Trouble is, this isn't ultimately about Israel. This isn't ultimately about Abraham. This isn't ultimately about Jerusalem.

This is about the King who promised to rule and reign from her hill. [17]

This is about the Savior who promised to impute His righteousness upon her soiled soul. [18]

This is about the God who promised to crush the head of the serpent for all our sake's. [19]

Ultimately, this is about His name. [20]

If we misunderstand or misrepresent Jerusalem, we misunderstand and misrepresent her—and our—Messiah.

---

17   See Psalm 2

18   Isaiah 46:13

19   Genesis 3:14-15

20   Deuteronomy 7:7-11; 9:6; Psalm 23:3; 25:11; 31:3; Ezekiel 20:44; 36:22; Acts 9:16

APPENDIX B

# GAZA AND THE GOSPEL OF

# THE KINGDOM

## AN OPEN LETTER TO MY FELLOW MILLENNIALS

*This article first appeared in
the* Covenant and Controversy
*online library,* [1] *May 2018*

Current events have a way of confronting what
we really believe to be true—rather, they have
a way of confronting us with what we really
believe to be true. The fourteenth of May in 1948
pressed us with what we'd really been reading
into Scripture's declarations; the redrawn
national borders of Israel continue to confront
us still. That fateful Friday in 1948 relit a slow-
burning powder keg of animosity; the last week
or two have set off fireworks—and we are, again,
confronted.

We're meant to be. [2]

---

1   Visit covenantandcontroversy.com for more

2   Zechariah 12:1-2

And we're found wanting.

Just before His Ascension, the disciples asked Jesus an earnest question: "Lord, will You now restore the Kingdom to Israel?" [3] How we read His answer could serve to suffice for how we'd distill the Gospel down to a sentence if need be.

> *Disciples*: "Lord, will You now restore the Kingdom to Israel?"
>
> *Jesus*: "It is not for you to know times or seasons that the Father has fixed by His own authority. But you will receive power when the Holy Spirit has come upon you, and you will be My witnesses in Jerusalem and in all Judea and Samaria, and to the end of the earth." [4]

It *really* matters for Palestinian people that we read this correctly. There runs a ditch on either side of the narrow road of truth, [5] and many are the victims to the numerous mudslides running through them. The straight and narrow is this: He did not rebuke them for asking the question. He just said, "The answer isn't yours to know. It's His. Right now, I have work for you to do."

"You will be My witnesses...."

Witnesses of what? Of "*this* Gospel of the Kingdom," the one Jesus so specifically referred

---

3   Acts 1:6

4   Acts 1:7

5   Matthew 7:13-14; see also pages 77-79

to just a month or more before. [6] Witnesses to where? "Everywhere, but start with the City of the Great King [7] and make your way through what many now call the West Bank. Hit Ramallah on your way to Doha. Hit Beirut on your way to Baghdad. Hit Gaza on your way to Guatemala. Go as far as you can on this round globe you call home, and go far enough that if you took one more step, because it's round, you'd start your journey home. Go to the ends of the earth."

Every Jewish ear within sonic range would've recognized Jesus' verbiage because they were familiar with the prophets—because they'd actually read and reread the Old Testament. They didn't disregard its implications or excuse away its prophecies. David sang about the ends of the earth. [8] Isaiah wrote at length about them. [9] Jeremiah chimed in. [10] Crucially, they would've understood what "this Gospel of the Kingdom" meant, because all their hopes were hanging on it. [11] They knew Jesus to be the Son of God, Man, and David, [12] and

---

6    Matthew 24:14, emphasis added

7    Psalm 48:2; Matthew 5:35

8    Psalm 2:8; 22:27; 48:10; 59:13; 65:5,8; 67:7; 72:8; 98:3

9    Isaiah 5:26; 24:14-16; 40:28; 41:5,9; 45:22; 52:10

10   Jeremiah 10:13; 16:19; 25:31; 51:16

11   Matthew 24:3; Luke 2:38; 3:15; Acts 1:6

12   Daniel 7:13; 8:17; Matthew 1:1,20; 8:20; 9:6,27; 10:23; 11:19; 12:23,40; 12:23; 13:37; 14:33; 15:22; 17:22; 19:28; 20:28-31; 21:9; 22:42; 24:27-29; 26:63-64; 27:40,43,54; Mark 1:1; 10:47-48; 13:26; 14:21,41,62; 15:39; Luke 1:35; 3:31,38; 11:30; 12:40; 17:24-30; 18:38-39; 19:10; John 1:34,49; 3:13-14;

they knew exactly why it is in everybody-since-Abraham's best interests that He rule and reign from the City of Peace. [13] They knew the "new song" of the "new covenant" would erupt from David's city and run across the nations until it hit New Zealand. [14] They knew it would make its way back until Muslims in Mecca and Amman bowed the knee to his Lord. [15] They knew the Arab world would be the last Gospel frontier before Jerusalem realized she killed her own Passover-preserved firstborn. [16] They knew the inauguration of the Davidic throne to be their "blessed hope," [17] and they were waiting for it.

"About this we have much to say, and it is hard to explain, since you have become dull of hearing." [18] I shudder to wonder what the author of Hebrews would say to us now if he could see what we've done with the name of Him who is greater than Moses, Melchizedek, and

---

5:27; 6:27; 9:35; 11:27; 12:23; 20:31

13    Genesis 12:1-3; 14:17-20 ("Salem" was an early name for "Jerusalem" and meant "peace"); 22:18; Psalm 110:4; Hebrews 5:6-10

14    See Isaiah 42:1-17

15    See Isaiah 42:11; Kedar refers to Arabia and Sela to Amman. David calling his Son his LORD: See Psalm 110:1; cited Matthew 22:44; Mark 12:36; Luke 20:42-43; Acts 2:34-35

16    See Exodus 12; Zechariah 12:10-14; Matthew 23:38

17    Titus 2:13; the Davidic throne is introduced in 2 Samuel 7 and noted again in 1 Chronicles 17:11-14 and 2 Chronicles 6:16; see Psalm 2; 110; 132. Psalm 110 is the most-quoted Old Testament passage in the New Testament, bearing significant witness to the apostles' prophetic anchor and bated hope in the reign of David's Son, a Man scripturally concurrent with the Messiah/Son of Man (see Daniel 7:13; 8:17) and Son of God (see note 11).

18    Hebrews 5:11

every king. [19] I shudder to wonder how Peter, Paul, or (especially!) Jesus would respond if we could time-travel back to this moment on the Mount called Olivet, raise our hands, and say, "Wait—You mean all that stuff Zechariah and Isaiah and Malachi and Micah and Hosea and Jeremiah and Daniel and David said is actually literal and legit and You're really gonna do it?"

> "You mean you're the teacher of Israel and you don't know these things? You need to be born again." [20]

What does this have to do with Gaza? And what does it mean for the Great Return March?

I was born in the eighties and grew up at least nominally affiliated with Christian culture. I was raised, christened, and nearly confirmed Catholic before entering Protestant evangelicalism just in time for the "if you like this demonic secular band then you should listen to this Nashville-crafted CCM substitute instead" posters and True Love Waits campaigns. The late nineties and early two thousands had a bizarre evangelical culture and I was *there for it*. I was there for the kissing-dating-goodbye and birth of ska (shout out to Five Iron!). And I was there for it when we all hit college and basically altogether left the faith (find your old youth group buddies on Facebook—who's still walking with the Lord?). I was there when the leaders of the "emergent

---

19    See Hebrews 1:8-9,13; 3:3-6; 4:14-10

20    See John 3, particularly verses 3 & 10

church" wrote a bunch of books to rewrite the Bible. I was there when we grappled with questions and realized we'd graduated high school with inch-deep theology and youth group faith. The world had problems, and we did not have answers—but we were determined to find them. "Social justice" became our buzzword and we seriously considered making our own clothes so we didn't have some kind of *Blood Diamond* situation with our blue jeans.

We didn't make our own clothes, but we read some books by some people who did.

We mostly didn't notice when they quoted Ghandi with the same sentiment they quoted Jesus.

The Israeli-Palestinian conflict confronts our glaring doctrinal inadequacy and missiological ineptitude. It pushes back on our cheap narratives and Twitter feed news intake. It challenges our historical ignorance. It holds the mirror up to those of us who are a generation removed from the ashes of the Shoah. We don't have Holocaust sympathies like our parents and grandparents did and far too many of us can't answer basic questions about its historicity. [21] Most of us can't answer basic questions about "this Gospel of the Kingdom." This is a problem, but we can't fix it if we don't address it.

---

21   Kelly, L. (2018). Shock poll: Two-thirds of millennials don't know what Auschwitz is. Washington Times, 12 April 2018. Retrieved from https://www.washingtontimes.com/news/2018/apr/12/many-americans-millennials-ignorant-holocaust-surv/

None of us want inch-deep theology and youth group faith. None of us want to author our own Gospel. And, none of us want to be sentimental, naive, Bible-ignorant hyper-Zionists who can't see the forest for the trees. No one wants to be complicit in supporting an aggressive, apartheid Jewish nation-state against the Palestinian people. I get it. Also, none of us want the wool pulled over our eyes by journalists who lie in order to live through their assignment. [22]

Intelligent information matters, but *The New York Times* isn't Bible and the only words we can really rely on are Bible. Doctrine matters—it *really* matters—but it's not the jugular issue. Jesus is the jugular issue. How we respond to something like the Great Return March or—heaven forbid—a Third Intifada is shaped and informed by what we believe the Gospel of the Kingdom to be, and who we believe Jesus of Nazareth to be in light of that. We've deviated from "this Gospel of the Kingdom" for so long, we can't recognize our glaring doctrinal and missiological insufficiencies when they stare us in the face.

Gaza and the #GreatReturnMarch are staring us in the face.

We have a biblical imperative to preach the Gospel to the Palestinian people, and we have a biblical imperative to preach the Gospel of the Kingdom

22    Friedman, M. (2018). Falling for Hamas's split-screen fallacy. *The New York Times*, 16 May 2018. Retrieved from https://www.nytimes.com/2018/05/16/opinion/hamas-israel-media-protests.html

when we do. We're under a Christ-imposed mandate to tell them about the little girl who gave it all for the Lord of the Resurrection. [23] This means we need to understand the Gospel, we need to understand the Kingdom, and we need to understand the Palestinians. We need to understand why Mary would waste it all at His feet. We need to understand Jesus like the prophets and the apostles understood Jesus. We need to understand Palestinian geopolitics and the Islamic worldview—and we need to understand it from the soil at the heart of Islam, instead of adopting a polished version of it from a community center in Detroit. We need to understand what Hamas is doing to the people of Gaza, and we need to care about it like we say we care about Israeli response to what we think are peaceful protests. And we need to evaluate if we really care about what we say we care about.

Ninety-nine-point-one percent of the Palestinian populous has not received a Gospel witness. [24] Nearly five million people live within Gaza and the West Bank, and 99.1 percent of them—99.1% of nearly five million people—are categorically unreached. Palestinian territories have an annual Gospel growth rate of precisely 0.0% [25]—so when our Twitter hashtags start trending some kind of #PrayForGaza solidarity sentiment, it

---

23    Matthew 26:13

24    Joshua Project. (2018). Country: West Bank/Gaza. Retrieved from https://joshuaproject.net/countries/WE 21 May 2018.

25    ibid.

is only that. It is only sentiment and it will be buried by the hashtag algorithm ten seconds later when something else goes viral. If we cared about the Palestinians, we'd get our feet on the ground and give them a Gospel witness. A Gospel witness is not a "kind humanitarian" witness. It includes that, but it is not limited to water distribution. It cannot be. [26] If we loved Jesus, we'd pour every drop of our blood and Bethany offering [27] out on the soil of the Promised Land if that's what it took to do something about the border fence. If that's what it took to bring Him back. [28]

If we do not sober up and have a collective "come to Jesus" moment, I'm not sure we're going to do the Middle East any good.

But believers are not debased, and we are not in the dark. [29] We are not bastard pagans. [30] We have a Father, and He is not unkind. Our Father is not unkind. He is the Father of mercies and lights. [31] He turned—and turns—the lights on for us. We have all the information we need. [32]

26   Matthew 10:42; Mark 9:41

27   See the account of Mary of Bethany anointing Jesus for His death and burial as recorded by Matthew (chapter 26), Mark (chapter 13), and John (chapter 12).

28   2 Peter 3:12

29   1 Thessalonians 5:4

30   Romans 8:15; Galatians 4:4-7

31   2 Corinthians 1:3; James 1:17

32   See Matthew 16 and "The Golan Heights & the Coming War to End All Wars" (https://www.youtube.com/watch?v=o7G-XB5AIW0&t=3s)

We do not need to live in delusion. Scripture equips and enables us to respond intelligently and compassionately to Jerusalem, Ramallah, and Gaza with a distilled Gospel-clarity, free from "sides" and narrative banners that only betray our own ignorance and unbelief.

We believe eternity to be real, or we don't. We believe justice to matter for the ages, or we don't. We believe sin to be high treason against our Maker, or we don't. We believe the Gospel premise that we're all sinners and we all deserve death, but Jesus in His magnificent mercy bore our sentence to die in order to make us forever alive, or we don't (this is true for us, for Palestinians, for Israelis—everybody). We believe God made promises to Abraham that really matter for all who call upon the God who raises the dead, or we don't. We believe David's Son deserves His throne and all war will cease when He sits upon it, [33] or I literally don't know what we're getting out of bed for in the morning. We believe the people of Gaza deserve "this Gospel of the Kingdom" and that Jesus is worth its declaration and their worship, or I have personally put my poor mother through far too much on this side of time and need to go home.

Gaza's going to hear this Gospel of the Kingdom. [34] Are you going to be part of it?

---

33    Psalm 46:9; 72:1-20; Isaiah 2:1-4; 9:7; Micah 4:1-5

34    Matthew 24:14

# ABOUT THE AUTHOR

Stephanie Quick is a writer and producer serving with Frontier Alliance International. She is the author of *Confronting Unbelief* and *To Trace a Rising Sun*, and a lead writer and producer contributing to the *Covenant and Controversy* film series and resource library. She lives in the Middle East and can be reached at stephanie@stephaniequick.org.

# ABOUT FAI

Frontier Alliance International is a missions organization devoted to exalting the worth of Jesus Christ among the unreached and unengaged at the end of the age. For more information on our relief, training, film, and publishing initiatives, visit faimission.org.

Because life is a vapor. Because death is gain. Because obedience. Because "do not take My Name in vain." Because life is Christ. Because faith. Because Gospel. Because it's for His glory's sake. Because the King will return. Because "the greatest of these is love." Because Psalm seventy-two. Because Revelation twenty-one. Because hope. Because this story isn't done. Because we're going to make plowshares out of all our swords and every gun. Because barrel bombs shouldn't fall. Because He took on flesh and blood. Because He said "go tell them all." Because He still does. Because nothing matters more than this. Because every nation needs a witness. Because the unreached deserve it. Because so many haven't heard yet. Because the manger. Because He knelt to wash our feet. Because grace. Because His blood still intercedes. Because the prophecies. Because Jerusalem and "blessed is He." Because it's not because He needs us. Because Zion.

# because Jesus.

89288022R00076

Made in the USA
San Bernardino, CA
26 September 2018